CW00495825

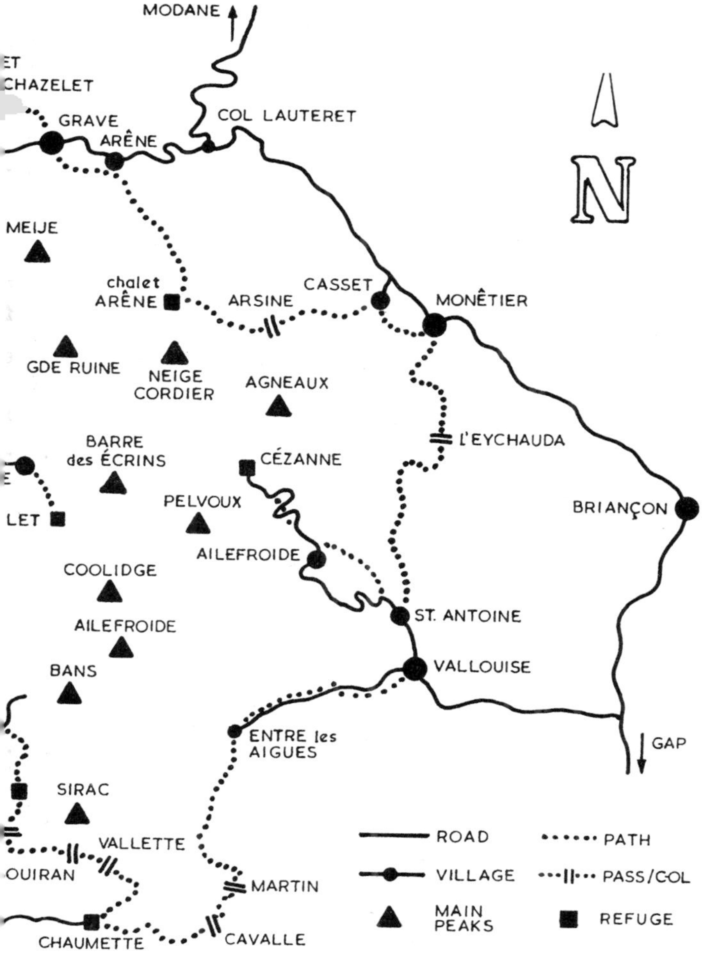
MODANE
ET
CHAZELET
GRAVE
ARÊNE
COL LAUTERET
N
MEIJE
chalet
ARÊNE
ARSINE
CASSET
MONÊTIER
GDE RUINE
NEIGE
CORDIER
AGNEAUX
L'EYCHAUDA
BARRE
des ÉCRINS
CÉZANNE
LET
PELVOUX
BRIANÇON
AILEFROIDE
COOLIDGE
ST. ANTOINE
AILEFROIDE
BANS
VALLOUISE
ENTRE les
AIGUES
GAP
SIRAC
VALLETTE
OUIRAN
MARTIN
CHAUMETTE
CAVALLE
ROAD
PATH
VILLAGE
PASS/COL
MAIN
PEAKS
REFUGE

TOUR OF THE OISANS

The TOUR de l'OISANS is the name given to one of the most strenuous alpine walks, fitting into the structure of French long-distance paths where it has been given the number 'GR54'. It is one of the routes which is circuitous, traditionally beginning and ending at the alpine resort of BOURG D'OISANS 40km (25 miles) to the east of Grenoble.

The massif it encircles is that of the Écrins, the bulk of which is a national park with tight restrictions imposed on the behaviour of its visitors, the aim of which is to conserve the environment with special emphasis on protecting the animal and plant life.

The landscape is stupendous. There are wondrous views to be had of the area and there is probably no spot along the whole route that lacks interest. The valleys through which the paths weave or cross are rich in individuality, the hamlets being varied in style and facility. Forest, meadows, bare mountainside, scree, scant tracks, stones, bushes, rocks, streams, pools, rivers, lakes, glaciers are the ingredients of the immediate environment and very little roadwork is encountered. Nearly everything along the way is at an angle, at some places very steep indeed.

The rivers and stream are amazingly clear, often to the point of translucence. You will discover elaborate waterfalls, some of which will be passed close at hand but others only to be admired from a distance.

TOUR OF THE OISANS
GR54:
A circular walk round
The Dauphine Alps

by

Andrew Harper

Photographs by the author

CICERONE PRESS
MILNTHORPE, CUMBRIA, ENGLAND

© ANDREW HARPER 1995
ISBN 1 85284 157 5
Published 1986
2nd Edition 1995

With thanks to Beryl Harper for the contour drawings, Jim Hartley for the sketches and both for their encouraging help.

Advice to Readers

Readers are advised that whilst every effort is taken by the author to ensure the accuracy of this guidebook, changes can occur which may affect the contents. It is advisable to check locally on transport, accommodation, shops etc. but even rights of way can be altered and, more especially overseas, paths can be eradicated by landslip, forest fires or changes of ownership.

The publisher would welcome notes of any such changes.

ANDREW HARPER is the author of the walking guide to the *Tour of Mont Blanc* - also published by Cicerone Press.

Front cover: Lac Noire and la Meije

CONTENTS

Path sign, Col de la Muzelle in background (day 10)

INTRODUCTION

GR54 should not be attempted by anyone who has not had a thorough 'primer' of approaching difficulty elsewhere in the Alps. The MONT BLANC TOUR is similar in scale: of distance and total ascended altitude, taking about the same time in which it can be accomplished. GR54 is arguably more difficult, being severe and exposed in places with attendant increase in danger and risk. Nevertheless, thousands flock to the area annually. The French quite rightly recognise its grand potential and there is a constant passage of people progressing their way around the paths.

The route ought to be punctuated by at least one rest day by staying at one of the villages through which GR54 passes. This would allow short excursions to be made with lighter packs or just simply to sit around, chat, write a few cards, attend to the laundry and ferret around the back lanes. Don't let it be constant hard work from beginning to end.

To race around the route in eight or nine days is feasible; there are those who may have done it in much less. But what a shame to make speed the aim. The author recalls the words of Walter Pause, who, in describing a walk in the Oberland, said: 'the CONNOISSEUR will always take a few days longer'.

The author has made many skirmishes into the area but it was only in 1984 that he made a dedicated visit and walked every path described in this book. Rather than write a hypothetical sectionalised description it was decided that the best approach would be to divide the route into 'days' which exactly relate to his own performance. On review, it was found to be one of the most rewarding routes attempted but, having said that, it was without doubt the most demanding.

The easier days of Five, Ten, Twelve and the 'day off' Eight were essential in balancing some very hard and long days which saved the holiday from being too punishing. Possibly as a result of this mixture the author had no ailment, no discomfiture, no feeling of excessive tiredness (slept well, though!) nor a single blister to contend with. He returned to work having felt the whole venture had done him good and not wanting 'another holiday' to recuperate.

Variations are possible to modify the itinerary described by the author, but will be limited in some cases by the opportunities of overnight accommodation.

Some people get an added satisfaction in doing the 'whole thing' in which case the aim will be to get back to the starting point eventually. This constraint means that buses, taxis, lifts and all other aids to progress will be shunned. However, excursions from the main route can be aided in this manner and an example is the bus journey to la Bérarde which will allow you to get a satisfactory impression of the place in just one day, whereas it would take three on foot.

If there is no desire to tread every pace of the route then some slight improvements can be effected. A minibus might be considered useful from Vallouise up to the roadhead at Entre-les-Aigues to make more effective progress. Another example might be to continue direct from Bourg d'Arud up the facing mountainside to Alpe-de-Venosc/Mont-de-Lans and on to Mizoën with all its open views, rather than proceed along the valley floor to reach Bourg d'Oisans. There's nothing wrong with the wooded path (in fact it is a very nice one) but the route over the mountains must surely be favoured. You may be fortunate in having the time available to do both and the book is written on that assumption.

The route may have to be varied due to landslips, problematic lying snow, works and other unforeseen obstacles. A certain versatility and judgement might have to be exercised. At the limit a route might have to be abandoned and common sense should play its part in making unfortunate decisions such as this.

The timings quoted are those taken by the author, all to the nearest five minutes. Quite often they are coincident with those seen elsewhere either in publications or on signs. They do not allow for halts of any kind.

Since 1984 the author has been able to visit the area on several more occasions and has seen for himself changes that have occurred in the meantime. Coupled with comments received from others, revision has become advisable and necessary, so this, the 2nd Edition embodies these changes.

SUMMARY

		ASCENT (METRES)	DESCENT (METRES)
Day 1	Bourg d'Oisans to Clavans le Bas	1,438	787
Day 2	Clavans le Bas to la Grave	1,270	1,157
Day 3	La Grave to Monêtier-les-Bains	1,065	1,051
Day 4	Monêtier-les-Bains to Ailefroide	1,227	1,216
Day 5	Ailefroide to ref. Cézanne, then Vallouise	374	714
Day 6	Vallouise to ref. Chaumette	1,654	1,030
Day 7	Ref. Chaumette to Chapelle-en-Valgaudemar	1,281	1,971
Day 8	- Day off -		
Day 9	Chapelle-en-Valgaudemar to le Désert	1,529	1,374
Day 10	Le Désert to Valsenestre	1,035	995
Day 11	Valsenestre to Bourg d'Arud	1,392	1,745
Day 12	Excursion to la Bérarde and ref. du Carrelet	197	197
Day 13	Bourg d'Arud to Bourg d'Oisans, including diversion to Brêche du Périer	1,670	1,895
		14,132	14,132
Day 14	Bourge d'Arud to Mizöen	858	614
Day 15	Mizoën to la Grave	1,490	1,195
		16,480	15,941
Day 16	Bourg d'Oisans to l'Alpe-d'Huez and return	1,138	1,138
		17,618 (57,802ft.)	17,079 (56,033ft.)

The 539m difference between the totals is explained as being the difference in the altitudes of Bourg d'Arud and la Grave.

From the sub total of 14,132m it is possible to calculate the total of ascent and descent for the basic tour starting and finishing at Bourg d'Oisans. This is done by deducting the excursion above St Antoine (Days 4 & 5), the excursion to la Bérarde (Day 12) and the diversion above la Danchère to Brêche du Périer (Day 13). This gives 11,709m and, being a circuit, the ascent and descent figures are the same (38,415ft).

The total distance is 305km (190 miles) of which the basic tour amounts to just 197km (123 miles).

GENERAL INFORMATION

WHEN TO GO

It seems that the likelihood of troublesome snow lying as late as mid-July determines the first time that the Tour de l'Oisans can be commenced. The days are long in July, but the weather conditions are notoriously 'wet'. August tends to be humid and muggy, but the first three weeks are to be avoided because the French vacation period is at its height. The influx of these Nationals will give your language studies an extra boost of 'practical' but don't underestimate their competition in securing bed-spaces. They thin out by about the 20th, so if you go then and spread into September there will be the additional benefit to be derived from low-season charges made by the hotels which come into force on the 1st of that month.

The sun rises about 7am and it starts to get dark about 7.30pm by early September, so the days are still long enough. The weather seems more settled, too. The end of September to mid-October can have its rewards, although the autumn shades don't establish themselves fully until mid-November. At that time of year one can walk all day and not see a soul - ideal if you are wanting solitude. The penalty for such a late visit will be that no refuge will be active and the valley hotels will have to be reached every night and probably they will have closed as well.

Summing up, then: 18th August to 16th September has, on average, all the advantages.

HOW TO GET THERE

The accepted starting point for attempting the Tour d'Oisans is Bourg d'Oisans, best described as a small mountain resort town which is some 40 miles from the city of Grenoble through which it is necessary to gain access to the region. Having arrived at Grenoble there is a bus service available for Bourg d'Oisans. There are many ways of getting to Grenoble, the most popular of which are:

1. By air to Geneva

Then take one of the frequent trains from the 'Aeroport' railway station to the City station, which takes some 5min. At the City station find the platform with its Frontier Control formalities for the services into France and, once off, the journey time to Grenoble can be as little as 2hr.

Be cautioned that the trains from Geneva to Grenoble are infrequent and are not necessarily phased to make an economic day. If one is just missed then the penalties of time wastage could become unacceptable. Trains from Lyon are more numerous, taking about 1hr10min.

2. By air to Lyon

Once at Lyon, you may find you have not long to wait for a bus that operates from there to Grenoble direct. Although the journey takes more time than by train, by the time you get to the City centre on the 'airport' bus and then wait for a train there would be little, if anything, in it - add to which it would be cheaper and more convenient.

3. By train from Paris

There are several services a day departing London to reach the French capital. Once there you would have to go to the station known as Gare de Lyon for your train to Grenoble. With the advent of their high-speed trains called 'TGV', the timetables are being revised so you should make enquiries nearer the date of your departure to ascertain their availability. Not only are there trains during the day but up to the middle of September there should be an overnight service.

4. By personal transport

Unless you are already versed in the mountain-road approaches to Bourg d'Oisans, you will probably come to Grenoble first. Depart Grenoble by the long and straight boulevard called 'Cours Jean Jaurès'. After what will seem an interminable number of traffic-light junctions, fork L at le Pont-de-Claix to reach Vizille. Follow signposted road to Bourg d'Oisans, the N91. There is a suitable public car park opposite the coach station at Bourg d'Oisans where your car could be left until you return for it at the end of the holiday.

Leaving a car for such a long time in a prominent public place will have its attendant risks. Others known to the author have found more peace of mind by continuing to the hamlet of le Châtelard (NE of Bourg d'Oisans) to park after negotiation with the inn keeper there. This provides an alternative and advantageous starting point, return at the end of the holiday being facilitated by bus from Bourg d'Oisans to Huez and utilising the linking paths via the Pont Romain.

5. By coach from London

Probably the cheapest method of reaching Grenoble is to make use of the 'Euroways' coach service operation from Victoria coach station. Details will be available from their main office at 52 Grosvenor Gardens, London SW1 (tel: 0171 730 0202). Departing mid-afternoon from London, the overnight journey is scheduled to arrive at Grenoble 'Gare Routière' (bus station) at 8am, but after such a long journey this should be regarded as an approximation.

Once at Grenoble

You will be invigorated by seeing 'mountains in every direction' when you get out into the fresh air at Grenoble, but no time should be lost in checking the times of the connecting bus (known to the French as *cars*) for Bourg d'Oisans and purchasing the appropriate ticket: this is accomplished in the 'Gare Routière' located outside the railway station. Note that on French bus services rucksacks are deemed as 'baggage' and can be charged, so it is advisable to declare that you have one when purchasing your ticket. The bus journey takes about 1½hrs.

Incidentally, the buffet at Grenoble station can be relied on for modestly-priced and satisfying self-service meals and snacks. Also, should it be necessary to stay in Grenoble overnight, the hotels opposite the station and in the surrounding streets are plentiful and not too pricey. Grenoble is a city of character and any time spent there can be gainfully employed by walking along the paved river bank and seeking the older part of the city with all of its interests.

INSURANCE

In keeping to the main paths you will stand the best chance of avoiding mishap. The ankle will always be at risk, though. With so much rock making up the environment it must be acknowledged that there is the remote possibility of a boulder bounding towards you: even stones dislodged by some thoughtless individual on a higher path can inflict painful consequences. Whilst the odds are in

Pont Romain

Balcony path after Col de Souchet (Day 2)
View above la Grave with la Meije (Day 3)

your favour for doing the whole Tour without mishap, injuries do occur.

Hospitalisation and medical care cost a lot of money, so for this reason you should consider taking out temporary cover by way of 'holiday insurance'. Ascertain that there is no clause which will absolve liability if policyholders are engaged in mountaineering pursuits. The author has been able to get cover from a company which draws the line only where the Alpine activity needs 'ropes or climbing aids'. When you get your policy, leave full details and a photostat copy with a relative or close friend and take the original with you.

There are reciprocal right available to you under the National Health Service arrangements, but you will have to approach your DHSS office to get details.

Take a whistle but before actually using it to summon assistance, do give very careful thought as to whether such a call needs to be made. Blowing whistles on mountainsides can be EXTREMELY expensive: the person being aided will subsequently have to bear all the costs of the rescue operation.

BASIC PRECAUTIONS FOR MOUNTAIN SAFETY

Ensure that you have adequate warm clothing.

Carry reserve supplies of food in case of difficulty.

Plan your day carefully, not overestimating your physical ability. Take into account the limitations imposed by the weakest or least experienced member of the party as well as being vigilant for anyone who might be showing signs of approaching ill-health.

Keep an ear open for weather forecasts, asking refuge guardians for their opinions about the prospects before departure. Keep an eye open for indications of worsening weather and be alert to the prospect of MIST closing in with little warning.

Don't hesitate to turn back or cut a section from your itinerary if the weather deteriorates. 'Pressing on' is folly and can sometimes lead to disastrous - even fatal - results.

It might prove helpful to consult the refuge guardian, police or even the hotelier by telling them where you intend to go. They are better placed to known about the state of the paths and give advice.

You will encounter some people who are walking the route in the opposite direction to yourself they are in the best position of all to advise and for this reason alone it often pays to have a chat with them before they pass.

In general, the best advice is to KEEP TO THE APPROVED PATHS. Stay together as a group and accept all the decisions made by the leader. Think ahead and make some plan for a rendezvous place and time should you get parted: even when separating to visit shops in the villages it can be extremely frustrating and a time-waster if there's some difficulty in meeting afterwards.

Know what to do in an emergency by reading such publications as *Safety on Mountains* published by the Central Council of Physical Recreation or the *Mountain Rescue Handbook* published by the Mountain Rescue Committee. These should be obtainable from most climbers' shops.

Never venture onto glaciers until you have first learned the special and necessary techniques.

Fatigue or slight injury can delay or halt progress and may mean a night in the open on high ground with attendant risk of exposure. The risk can be lessened to a large degree by carrying a 'survival bag', although if you find yourself without one a conventional dodge is to empty your rucksack and then draw it up over feet and legs. Put on all the clothing you can at an early stage and aim to keep head, hands and feet as warm as possible. You will of course take the best advantage of any shelter that may avail itself, getting into a position that offers the best protection from any wind.

For those who disregard precautions, the onset of bad weather can mean acute physical discomfort, loss of direction, growing fear and even collapse. The surest defence against these dangers is the observance of all the mountain safety procedures.

Should it come to it and you want to summon assistance then the recognised signalling pattern is by whistle, lamp or voice. Six long blasts, flashes or yells for one minute, followed by one minute of silence. Then repeat. The spaces of each alternative minute are to permit reply which will consist of three blasts.

This list of precautions would not be complete without reminding you about the value of the compass. Carrying one is not an effective answer unless you've acquainted yourself in how it should be used. One of its best applications is to continually up-date its setting for the general directions of travel, particularly if mist threatens. An indispensable item.

THE REFUGES

It is very difficult to make reservations in advance and even if this is achieved a booking will not be held for an extremely late arrival. A disadvantage with booking is surely that the walker is tied to making a particular landfall each day, running the danger in so doing of outreaching his capabilities. Far better to have flexibility of manoeuvre and allow the odd-day tolerance for rest, sightseeing or to sit-out bad weather without being under an obligation to press on. It is best, really, to proceed as far as you are able each day aiming to arrive at a place where accommodation is normally available. Reckon to approach early - this is the surest way of guaranteeing a place, although finding the refuge full to the seams with a school party can be terribly disheartening.

Newcomers to the mountains are often uncertain as to the formalities involved in gaining access to refuges. They all tend to have their own character and a lot depends on the personality of the guardian, who sometimes takes residence with his family for the season. At a lot of them, all the produce used in supplying the meals has to be carried up from the valley by the guardian, so be patient if the refuge you are at is an example of this and be tolerant of the restricted menu. At some refuges the guardian might only prepare a meal for you if the major ingredient (meat or whatever) is given to him by the visitor. Towards the end of the season you may even find a refuge unattended, so allow for this eventuality by carrying at the least some soup powder. There is normally provision made for self-cooking and an area set aside for this, usually with pans, crockery and cutlery. A small fee is levied for the use of this facility.

Membership of an organisation is not essential although there are advantages such as reduction in charges for stays in their refuges and priority of admission. However, if you do the sums, you will doubtless find that the savings will not outweigh the expense of membership.

When you arrive, make yourself known immediately to the guardian and tell him of your requirements.

The basic type of sleeping arrangement found in the refuges has dormitory-style bedding where mattresses are laid side-by-side with a pillow and two blankets allocated to each space. The sexes are not usually segregated. Keep your torch handy so that any move from the bedspace during the hours of darkness can be made manageable through the heap of rucksacks, pitons, crampons, ice-axes, sticks and discarded clothing. You will notice that boots weren't quoted in the list: they would have been compulsorily deposited in the lobby area, where ungainly plastic plimsolls are available to the visitor.

Few premises have bedrooms as such, but quite often the dormitory accommodation is divided into rooms of varying size. Obviously, the smaller number of people sleeping in any one room will increase the likelihood of an undisturbed night. Bunk-beds are a familiar feature, where the restless occupant usually influences the slumber of the others.

It would seem that the guardians each have authority to end their season depending on the circumstances and fall in demand. You should always be prepared to find a refuge closed, even though told otherwise as you passed through the preceding village. In such an eventuality, don't overlook the strong likelihood of a 'winter room' being open: quite often access is through an unimposing door you might otherwise not attempt to open. Bare necessities would then generally be available to you.

The following refuges are on the itinerary:

le Toit Pointu	(Day Two)
Villar d'Arêne	(Day Three)
Cézanne	(Day Five)
Pré de la Chaumette	(Day Six)
Vallonpierre	(Day Seven)
Souffles	(Day Nine)
Muzelle	(Day Eleven)
du Carrelet	(Day Twelve)
du Fay	(Day Fifteen)

GÎTES and GÎTE D'ÉTAPES

The original interpretation of the word *gîte* described a shepherd's cottage, but if this is what they were then they have been converted or created to offer 'holiday' accommodation, usually booked by families for several days at a time. A *gîte d'étape* is more of a transit hostel although this longer descriptive name is often confusingly abbreviated to 'gîte'. Both the *gîte* and the *gîte d'étape* will be encountered on the GR54, but it will be the *gîte d'étape* that will generally be of service.

Run on simple lines, often without a resident guardian, *gîte d'étapes* normally have an evening meal available. In many ways they are indistinguishable from refuges but are usually only situated in the villages. It appears that they are constructed from an otherwise unwanted building although some are purpose-built. Of obvious benefit to the rambler, their presence plays an important part in the staging of the GR54. Of advantage to the villagers, these premises concentrate the daily influx of passing walkers into the one controllable lodging, freeing the traditional establishments to continue their normal trade with the motorist and the well-attired.

Gîte d'étapes are established at:

Bourg d'Oisans	(Day One, Day Thirteen, Day Fifteen)
Clavans-le-Bas	(Day One)
Besse-en-Oisans	(Day Two)
la Grave	(Day Two)
Villar d'Arêne	(Day Three)
Casset	(Day Three)
Ailefroide	(Day Four)
Vallouise	(Day Five)
Chapelle-en-Valgaudemar	(Day Seven)
Villar-Loubière	(Day Eight or Nine)
le Désert	(Day Nine)
Valsenestre	(Day Ten)
la Bérarde	(Day Twelve)
Venosc	(Day Fourteen)
Mizoën	(Day Fourteen)

DORTOIRS

These are rooms either in a building built for the purpose or in, say, an attic or annexe at a hotel where bedding and washing/toilet facilities exist at very reasonable prices. They are similar in many ways to a *gîte d'étape*, but tend to be managed by a hotel or restaurant with which it is either joined or placed quite nearby. The phrase *avez vous le dortoir, s'il vous plaît?* often produces a room which might not otherwise have been offered. The prices charged are usually extremely economic.

OTHER PLACES TO STAY

List of accommodation can be obtained by writing to the local Offices, but delay your enquiry until early April as an earlier approach may bring forth their winter tariffs complete with information about skiing holidays! Undeniably it is reassuring to have a hotel list in your pocket for the odd occasion when you stride into a village late one evening, but provided you can reach the Tourist Office before it closes - about 5.30 it seems - then they will be able to sense your requirements on the spot and tell you what is available, often saving a needless search at the end of a tiring day. Even when closed, some have the hotel situation displayed outside their premises to facilitate your selection. At the extreme, the effects of a bad choice will only last one night; it is not as though you will be committing yourself to a fortnight's stay.

It is quite common to find bedrooms equipped for two persons with the price quoted 'per room' and it may be that a stay under such conditions will prove economical. If your aim is to save money, then don't have the preconceived idea that older places offer the cheapest terms - quite often the author has been amazed at the reasonable tariffs associated with recently-constructed hotels. Prices invariably include the 'continental' breakfast, although there will be times when you may feel that it was hardly worth waiting for. At many places it is not available until 8am - later on Sundays - and a valuable part of the day will have been lost in waiting for it. You may well consider that it would be far better to try to buy a fresh loaf or acquire some bread to have with some jam and to make a little headway before preparing some coffee of your own.

When registering at each place of stay you may be asked to complete a simple questionnaire: a statutory requirement, but a nuisance all the same. At some hotels you might be made to surrender your passport for the period of stay. Be encouraged to settle your account just before retiring to bed on the eve of your departure as this will save a needless wait in the morning until a responsible member of the management puts in an appearance.

At a campsite the Camping Carnet is the more usual document sought but whether it is this or a passport do remember not to leave without it.

BACKPACKING

This form of travel has a lot to recommend it and there is no denying that it overcomes the need to make certain landfalls each evening in order to secure traditional accommodation. It follows from this that there could be a more efficient way of dividing the Tour. Backpacking has to be the solution when planning an expedition to an area where there is NO accommodation, but, as there are plenty of places to stop you are not forced to do it. Don't invest in backpacking equipment just for the sake of it, as the penalty of increased weight may make the GR54 into an unnecessary exercise of labour and lessen the enjoyment.

There seem to be no real restrictions against pitching tents above the treeline outside the National Park boundaries but you should be advised to utilize the provided sites whenever possible. Within the National Park, only bivouacing is permitted and then at a point that would be more than two hours march to an exit. In addition, the circumstances must be that the walker is caught by storm or troubled by injury. Their definition of a bivouac is where the tent size is such that the occupant cannot stand upright inside it. It cannot be assembled until after sunset and must be dismantled before sunrise.

The author prefers a degree of independence and managed to sleep in his Saunders' 'Jetpacker' for a total of eleven blissful nights, none of which was within the National Park boundaries and only three of which happened to be on recognised sites.

SLEEPING BAGS

Established backpackers will already have their favourite brand of bag, chosen as much for its packed size and weight as for its thermal insulation. But - if you're not backpacking - do you really need one? *Gîte d'étapes* tend to be at lower altitudes than the refuges but, even in these, it can sometimes get miserably cold and there are bound to be times when you wish you had that little bit of extra protection to snuggle into. Just think of the situation in a crowded refuge where there is absolutely no alternative than to sleep on the floor of the entrance lobby! Obtain one if you can but, as you'll have it for many such holidays, be prepared to pay a little extra to get one that packs small and will be light to carry.

CLOTHING AND GEAR

There is one basic difference between fellwalking in Britain and walking the route described in this book: the temperature can change by as much as 20°C in as many minutes, the effect of which is made worse by a vanishing sun. This would be an extreme possibility. The author hopes that your holiday will be free of bad weather with continual clear visibility but it is his duty to warn you that such perfection is rare. A good philosophy is to EXPECT bad weather, then, if it comes, it won't feel so bad and the demoralising effect will be minimised. If good weather shows itself then just regard that as a bonus!

The paths trod are quite often the highest paths in the area and with increased height it can be assumed that dangers due to weather increase also. Take warm clothing such as thick shirts, substantial trousers, a windproof jacket or anorak, woollen cap that can be pulled down over the ears, socks in good condition. Gloves are essential but they must be protected by waterproof 'overgloves' or made from some composite material. A scarf will be little weight to add when you consider its potential value. Mountain walkers often prefer to take two thin pullovers so that they can be donned or removed to the requirements of the moment as distinct from the all-or-nothing 'chunky' sweater.

Boots are a 'must' and the selection of these will be based on individual preference - they should not only repel water but be in a state of good repair. Make certain there is plenty of room for the toes and that they fit snugly at the ankles. Of course, new boots should be 'run in' prior to departure and any adjustments made in good time. Don't forget to take a spare lace. You may care to take a pair of plimsolls to relax into as chances occur, but, in any case, you will want something like this for the hotels and refuges. Anklets can come in handy, their main service being to prevent small stones entering the boot. Leggings are really not necessary but they are a godsend if there's a lot of deep snow to trudge through. Ropes and crampons are considered unnecessary, but, here again, there could be just that awkward pitch of 50ft or so of icy slope that would make them indispensable.

Rainwear in the form of a jacket or cagoule plus overtrousers should be 100% efficient in combating continual rainfall but good sunglasses and a peaked cap will help overcome the problems associated with the weather when it turns its other cheek. Good quality 'glacier' cream should be applied to nose, lips and the tops of ears as a precaution rather than a cure and if it gets very hot a thin cotton shirt worn with shorts will make you feel much cooler.

The rucksack should ideally be of such a capacity that it just comfortably holds the maximum you wish to carry that is not actually being worn. Don't plan to strap your jacket on the outside but make sure there will be room for it within. Too loose a rucksack can be uncontrollable and become a nuisance. Side pockets are useful for the water container and small items on general call like the camera and washing gear. Aim to keep it as light in weight as possible to the point of being ruthless. Remember that whatever style of pack you decide upon, it will be with you throughout every pace so don't be hurried into buying a design that is not going to prove suitable.

A little washing powder will be useful, but having washed your clothes it becomes a problem to dry them thoroughly. A good tip is to take a few safety pins and use them to fasten the items onto the outside of the rucksack as you march along - even then it can take a whole day for thick socks to dry. Take a modest-sized torch, such that the battery stands an even chance of outlasting frequent short bursts of use. Another useful thing to take is a foam rubber cushion (about 8"x12"x1$^{1/2}$") covered in thin material: this will act as an additional pillow in the train or refuges, take the sting out of lunch-break halts and protect your camera should you happen to fall or drop your rucksack.

Finally in this list of suggestions - plenty of thin plastic bags. These will be useful for all kinds of food, not only keeping perishables fresh for longer but saving the other contents in the sack from contamination by spilt liquids, split tomatoes, etc. Bread will 'survive' for days if additionally placed in a large polythene bag. Wrapping clothes in these bags has double value: preventing dampness reaching things you want to keep dry as well as giving neater and smaller things to stow.

WATER

You will surely take a water container and this will become part of your lifeline for days on end. It will be of additional comfort if it is designed so that you can drink directly from it and has an efficient screw cap which does not weep. Make sure you fill up before leaving your hotel/refuge, although you will encounter many standpipes. If the water is unsuitable, there is usually a prominently-placed notice to that effect: l'EAU NON POTABLE. Most of the streams seem harmless enough, but you will have to make your own decisions about that. There are proprietary tablets available that can be added to water - these seem to work on the basis of chlorination. If having added them you cannot taste the chlorine then you must add another until you do.

A small butane stove will be of value in brewing-up for tea, coffee and the occasional soup. One 90gm cartridge per person per week seems to be the way it works out, provided an effective attempt has been made to screen the flame. The screw-top self-sealing canister does not appear to be available in France, whereas the pierceable 'Gaz' is on sale readily both in the 190gm and 90gm sizes. If you are travelling by air, be cautioned that the conveyance of these cartridges is STRICTLY FORBIDDEN and so you will have to equip your stove on arrival. 'Gaz' is on sale in Geneva near to the railway station at a large store called 'PLACETTE' in their sports department on 4th floor. The supermarket and other shops in Bourg d'Oisans stock them as well as the other villages you will be passing through.

The lighting of fires is prohibited within the National Park, but stoves of the 'Camping Gaz' type are permitted. Pay particular attention as to how you discard your matches and be sure that the cooker is positioned firmly where there is not the slightest chance of it causing harm.

COSTS

It would be nice to be able to give examples of costs so that it would be easier to budget for the expenses of the holiday but as prices invariably increase from year to year, aggravated by fluctuating exchange rates, any examples would inevitably and quickly become invalid and outdated.

CURRENCY

Fortunately the Tour is conducted wholly within France and therefore only French francs will be needed, although if the approach is through Geneva then do allow adequate Swiss currency for the short journeys within the town and any meals or a hotel that might be needed there.

More often than not, settling accounts as you progress the GR54 will be at modest establishments and the general recommendation is to have your stock of currency made up of small denomination notes, 100 franc French notes being particularly suitable. Having larger will chance the risk of being short-changed, whether intentional or not! Incidentally the word *monnaie* (pronounced much as our word 'money') relates to coinage, whereas the notes are referred to as *argent*. Their word *change* relates to currency exchange and not **coinage**.

Eurocheque cards and their associated cheques are becoming increasingly popular although travellers' cheques can still be beneficial in carrying currency reserves. Cashing travellers' cheques can be a problem due to the limited opportunities and several visitors to the area have experienced difficulty in getting them cashed. Even when in the right place you might not find it convenient to be there at the right time!

Credit cards are hesitantly accepted at some venues, but, surprisingly, some hotels in the region will not accept them as a form of payment so if you intend to settle your bill by this method you ought to verify if you can.

MAPS

Massifs Écrins Haut Dauphiné 1:50,000 Didier & Richard (D&R)
Massifs des Écrins 1:25,000 Institut Géographique National (IGN) Nos. 241, 242 and 243.

The 50,000 is an adequate map for accompanying the walker. It could benefit from being cut into, say, three smaller and more convenient strips - discarding the quite large areas of it that are not pertinent. The three 25,000 maps are easier to interpret but might have their proper place at the planning stage rather than add bulk to the load carried.

Should you encounter difficulty in obtaining your maps, then the following specialist will be in a position to supply:

Edward Stanford Ltd.,
12 Long Acre,
London WC2E 9L

The Map Shop,
15 High Street,
Upton-upon-Severn,
Worcs. WR8 0HJ

Be on the lookout for a huge 1:50,000 model map of the whole area which can be found on display in most Tourist Offices and the occasional hotel, refuge or restaurant. They make fascinating study and will give you a much clearer appreciation of the lie of the land.

You will find that place names are sometimes spelt in different ways, even on adjacent signs! There are examples of these discrepancies within reference pamphlets and other documents, too. Whether or not there is an 'accent' can introduce yet another variable. Trying to rationalise them is a risky pastime, so the 1:25,000 maps have been adopted as the authoritative source for the production of this book.

WAYMARKS

The basic waymark for the area is a red stripe with a white one next to it, usually horizontal. They are to be found on tree trunks, posts, on path-side rocks, even on the roadway surface. In some villages there are several painted on successive buildings to steer the walker through. At places the paint brush has simply scrawled 'GR54' or 'GR'. Occasionally you will see a very elaborately produced sign, either a metal casting or carved from wood.

Whilst the short parallel red/white stripes are those most commonly seen, occasionally they are found 'kinked', almost an inverted 'L'. This would be warning of an impending turn and is a prompter to watch for the change in direction. Should you see the red/white lines forming a cross, then this is an indication that you have come the wrong way and must go back a little to seek the correct path.

Waymarking is a desirable feature for any mountain walk, particularly if in unfamiliar territory, and has its greatest value in conditions of restricted visibility. Too often there is no sign or mark at all, frequently at a junction where a bit of guidance would be welcomed and appreciated. Neither is there a wholehearted policy to label the cols as only a few are accorded this courtesy.

Some valleys seem to have their own pride in maintaining clear and prominent waymarks and they are obviously to be complimented. However, the situation is such that there would have to be a lot of waymarking done along the GR54 before anyone could dare claim it as being perfect. Still, it would be naïve to depend on the presence of these signs to steer you round the course: fortunately no continuous guiderail is needed to complete the Tour successfully and pathfinding is not unduly difficult.

PHOTOGRAPHY

There is probably nothing better than a large-format, ie. 5" x 4", camera to do the Alpine scene justice. However, weight and space demand equipment of lighter and more manageable dimension.

35mm-format cameras are the most practical, giving very acceptable results. You can look at the colour pages of most mountaineering magazines and be assured that the majority of these pictures started life in that way. The single-lens reflex versions have two advantages over their cousins inasmuch as picture-framing is accurate and the by-product of exchangeable lenses is undeniably an asset. A 28mm lens seems to 'paint a picture', whereas a 100mm or 135mm will be useful for closer studies of the peaks or more distant features.

On recent holidays the author has used a Minox 'GT', the smallest, most expensive and probably the best of the 'compacts'. It is so small and light, slipping into the pocket unobtrusively. Taking 35mm film, its results are of the highest order and its fixed 35mm lens produces a pleasing aspect to the scenery. It has an immaculate self-timer and being aperture-priority in its operation, allows very accurate, lengthy exposure times in dark situations.

Colour reversal (transparency) film gives the best results but, unless they are printed in a book or magazine, they can only be viewed by projection, although there is a process gaining favour which will make superb colour prints directly from the transparency. Black and white film is still claimed by some dedicated photographers to give the most 'feeling' and 'atmosphere', additionally allowing manipulation in the darkroom to modify the effects and the framing. Colour negative has the convenience of readily producing prints of good quality - these are the most convenient for showing friends and relatives, but quite often they cannot contain the contrast range imposed, resulting in some lack of detail in the brighter areas.

25 or 64 ASA film will usually be found to be quite suitable for the anticipated lighting conditions. The use of a 'skylight' or 'UV' filter is encouraged. Some form of camera support will be invaluable at times, but the use of a full-height tripod is generally ruled out because of its unmanageable shape when it comes to transportation. Please do not disturb or frighten any animal with your photographic attempts - this is a Park regulation - nor must flowers or plants be damaged.

THE LANGUAGE

There is a general claim that 'they all speak English'. Let the author assure you that THEY don't! On his walk he reckoned only to chance upon two who spoke English to an acceptable degree of competence and remembers only another five or six whose command of the language bordered on being incoherent. It is surprising how even a little knowledge of French can see you through the most bizarre situation, but obviously the more fluent one becomes then the communication barrier eases in proportion.

In the absence of any knowledge of the language, how about following one of the BBC TV or radio courses? These are usually backed-up by discs or cassettes that can be purchased along with an informative booklet that gives additional explanations and practice opportunities. Making such a purchase would allow you to proceed with the study at your own pace and you will probably become impressed with your progress.

An English/French dictionary is all but useless as it will be rare to find someone who is tolerant enough to wait while you find the words needed to convey your message. A phrasebook is a good compromise, but finding your way through those when under pressure will not be all that easy. Their best use comes at mealtimes when you should have ample opportunity to dwell on the task of seeking the names of the foods and drink. Still beer is *bière* and steak is *steack* so the essentials are already known to you. But don't jump at the similarity of some of their words to solve your translation problems. For instance, a menu in Britain means the list of dishes on offer. Their word for that is *carte*. *Menu* refers to 'the meal of the day' or 'set meal'. The phrase for a boiled egg (a simple and readily available snack there) eluded the author for years. It is simply *un oeuf à la coque* ('egg in the shell').

Repas will be a word you will encounter, particularly in places in which you might be staying, and this relates to basic meals which will 're-fortify': *p.d.* is the oft-seen abbreviation for *petit dejeuner*, the basic breakfast which normally comprises a roll or bread with jam and choice of beverages (usually coffee or tea, sometimes hot chocolate), occasionally served with fruit juice and/or a limited selection of cheese.

TELEPHONE

Nearly every telephone call-box you encounter should have the ability to permit direct-dialling to the UK. First lift the handset and then insert two or three 1-franc pieces into the coin box. Resist the temptation to use the higher value coins as in the case of a 'wrong number' you would unnecessarily lose too much money. Then wait for dialling tone. Most public telephones now require phone cards which may be purchased from newsagents,etc.

Dial 19 - Wait for fresh/different tone
Dial 44
Dial STD code of number you require WITHOUT the first 0.
Dial the number of your UK party.

The author has found that it is not good policy to allow a hotelier to get the number for you or to allow you to use a phone, whose charge will appear on your account. The charges levied have been invariably much, much higher than for the same length of call made in a public box. Their PTT offices have a facility that has no equal in the UK, namely a metered telephone system where the charges are precise: present yourself at one of the counters and indicate your wish to use the telephone. The clerk will tell you which cubicle to occupy when you can make a stream of calls and then pay according to his meter reading. Unless they are extremely busy, they will offer assistance in obtained a number for you.

SNAKES

In the region there are two types of snakes and, unfortunately, one of them is venomous: the viper. Usually very dark green (some so dark as to appear black), they have zig-zag stripes characterising the upper surface of their short length. The good news is that they are timid and it is rare to see even one, although the author chanced upon a most magnificent specimen in the vicinity of lac Lauvitel (Day 13).

The other is known locally as the Couleuvre. By comparison with the viper, it is brightly coloured and is normally much bigger.

ADDITIONAL INFORMATION

The Parc National des Écrins has its administrative offices at:

Parc National des Écrins,
Maison du Parc, 05290 VALLOUISE,
Hautes Alpes, France

which is interesting, because of all the information sought prior to

Path to Ref. des Souffles (day 9)

Refuge de l'Alpe de Villar d'Arêne (Day 3)
Refuge Xavier Blanc (Day 7)

the author's visit theirs was the most scant. In addition, as you will see for yourself, the waymarking in the valleys associated with Vallouise is distinguished by its absence.

By far the best response came from:

Parc National des ÉCRINS, Secteur Briançonnais,
35 Avenue du Lauteret,
05100 BRIANÇON,
Hautes Alpes, France

who sent a pleasant, full and encouraging letter with no less than thirteen comprehensive and informative leaflets that ranged from a list of refuges to a study of ant life. All in the French language, but useful and interesting nevertheless.

When applying for information it would be courteous to send an International Reply Coupon which can be purchased from all UK post offices. If writing to Briançon, then 3 Coupons might be more appropriate as a going rate if you are hoping to get the same quantity of information as that received by the author.

The head office for the GTA/CIMES (the organising committee for long-distance footpaths in the French Alps) is at:

GTA/CIMES Maison du Tourisme,
14 Rue de la République, BP 227,
38019 GRENOBLE cedex,
Hautes Alpes, France.

However, several approaches in person and various enquiries by correspondence have amounted to little. Their replies have been ineffectual and unsupported by even the most basic leaflet.

Don't overlook a general enquiry to:

French Government Tourist Office,
178 Piccadilly, London W1V 0AL

which can provide general information and answer particular queries although train enquiries must be made at the Information Offices of British Rail.

BON VOYAGE!

The author hopes you have a particularly successful and pleasant time in the area of the Écrins. Subsequently you might come to regard it as one of the best holidays you have had and be tempted to return again and again.

Clavans-le-Haut seen from Col de Sarenne

DAY ONE
Bourg d'Oisans to Clavans le Bas

BOURG d'OISANS - numerous hotels, restaurants, bars, shops, PTT (post office), several camping sites, gîte d'étape (hostel). A thriving community situated symmetrically in a flat plain hemmed in by what appear at first sight to be sheer mountainsides. Buses come here from Grenoble and continue via la Grave to Monêtier-les-Bains and Briançon as well as the two major ski resorts of l'Alpe-d'Huez and les Deux Alpes. A minibus runs to la Bérarde calling at Venosc and Bourg d'Arud on its way there.

The road coming from Grenoble and Vizille sweeps to the left through the centre of Bourg d'Oisans and it is in this direction that the walk commences. The buildings and housing noticeably thin out and on the left will be found a supermarket which might be of service. Further down the road the bridge spanning the river Romanche will be crossed. The road towards la Grave/col Lauteret turns sharply to the right but you must choose the slip road to the left which will be signposted as going towards l'Alpe-d'Huez. Follow the road along the floor of the valley until it reaches an area devoted to three large campsites.

The path commences immediately before a bridge, leaving the roadway at the far end of the 'Camping la Cascade' site. The first red/white waymark will be observed on an electricity pylon just there.

The path is obvious but after about fifteen minutes take care not to miss a sharp junction to the R which must be taken. It is all too easy to be distracted by the gorge on the L and go past the turning. If you find the path narrowing and closing towards the water at the foot of the gorge then return to seek the proper turn off. The correct path skirts over bare, smooth rocks to give good views back towards Bourg d'Oisans but it soon gets amidst trees and shrubs to gain height. You will come onto a narrow road when getting to the few

DAY ONE
BOURG D'OISANS to CLAVANS LE BAS

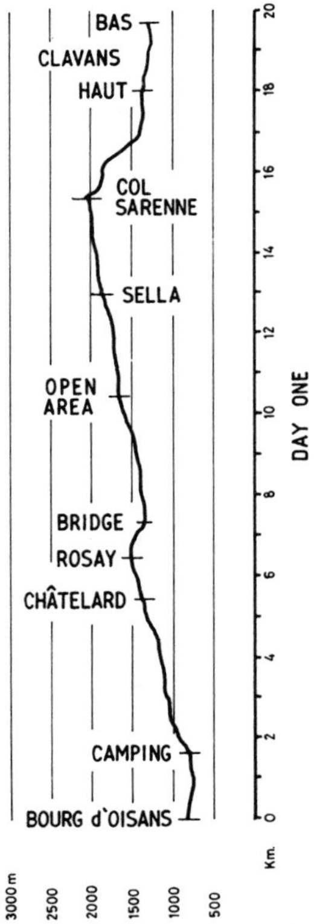

DAY ONE
BOURG D'OISANS to CLAVANS LE BAS
8h. 15m 20km.

	Timings		Altitude in metres	Ascent & Descent
	Sectional	Accumulative		
BOURG D'OISANS			717	
	0.20	0.20		+ 12 − 6
CAMPSITES			723	
	1.10	1.30		+332 − 24
La Ville			1031	
	1.05	2.35		+450 − 33
le CHÂTELARD			1448	
	0.15	2.50		+ 52
le ROSAY			1550	
	0.45	3.35		+ 7 − 83
Bridge			1424	
	1.00	4.35		+236
Path Junction			1660	
	0.40	5.15		+170
Bridge/Chlt. du SELLA			1830	
	0.50	6.05		+179
Col de SARENNE			2009	
	1.50	7.55		−602
CLAVANS le HAUT			1407	
	0.20	8.15		− 39
CLAVANS le BAS			1368	

Total ascent: 1438
descent: 787

buildings at **la Ville**. Take care to turn R immediately past the large building (it has a tall latticed radio mast alongside) and proceed straight across another small road a few paces later.

The inclination from here is fairly constant and with the hours beginning to pass the effect of increased sunshine will be lessened due to the shading caused by the trees through which the path penetrates. About here the rucksack straps will probably be beginning to make their presence known, threatening to cut into the shoulders with their unfamiliar load! Relief comes at **le Châtelard** where the path first breaks out into the open providing clear views over the divide towards the village of Huez-en-Oisans which is some distance up the zig-zagging road reaching towards l'Alpe-d'Huez. Soon the few buildings are reached, one obviously an active hotel which offers sandwiches and liquid stimulants that may be timely upon your arrival. The author reached this place as it was approaching noon, finding preparations under way in the restaurant to serve lunches to other visitors. Sitting in the shade at one of the outside tables with a bottled beer to accompany the Sainsbury's individual meat pie was all that was necessary on this occasion and the break was worthwhile. Take the metalled road which skirts the hillside to pass Maronne and reach **le Rosay** but remember to fork R off it immediately prior to the village. You will now be on a path and you must fork L just past the housing. This leads to an extremely pleasant pasture before beginning to lose altitude down a rocky escarpment (safe, but take care!) until reaching a wee stone bridge that you'll find set amongst dense trees.

Once over the bridge, turn R onto a path that has come from the village of Huez. This gains height gradually, eventually coming to a Y-junction where a coin can be flipped to decide on which side of the river to continue as both paths come together at another small bridge some 20min further on. Here will be found a clearing which houses the Auberge de la Combe Haute, a café/bar offering midday meals and accommodation on a dortoir basis.

Continue on the same side of the river as the Auberge and soon you will emerge above the tree-line into an enormous clearing, divided only by the attractive water flow of the young river Sarenne where you might be tempted to rest awhile, brew-up, bathe the feet?

Continue straight on through a narrow defile and much further until encountering a bridge at a nondescript place called **Chalet du Sella**. Very dusty underfoot on this stretch and the slightest breeze will whisk this into the air and make the going somewhat unpleasant. Go half-R at the bridge and head cross-country to short-cut the jeep track that, like you, is heading for **COL de SARENNE**.

The grassy terrain that leads to the pass is replaced by a landscape of rock on the other side. Follow the road over and new broader views will appear. After a short while you will be able to see right down to the valley bottom where the cluster of shining roofs represent the village of Clavans le Haut, your next target. Fortunately you will not have to plod the whole length of the roadway that can be seen sweeping the broad width of the hillside as, after a couple of hairpins, a path goes off and down to the R. This will quickly stress the ankles and it seems to go interminably downwards long after the calf muscles have screamed their displeasure.

Things ease eventually where you can see a sign pointing back the way you've just come: FACILE, the French word for 'easy'. What can be 'difficult' then? Wait until later and you will get the answer! Go over the road straight into a mule track that immediately swings to the R to lead into **Clavans le Haut**. A likeable place with very attractive old buildings but not one of them a restaurant or bar, although water is plentiful at the fountain.

Once through the village, take the RH fork in the road and follow it up to its first bend where the path will be found going off to the left and which can then be followed all the way to **CLAVANS le BAS**.

Not to be confused with the active gîte in le Bas (which is available only for private booking), the gîte d'étape was closed when the author passed in 1993 and it is anyone's guess if it will ever re-open. This forces those in need of accommodation to continue to Besse where ample facilities will be found to exist, although this will add significantly to the length of the day's walk.

Before leaving the description for Day One, consideration ought to be given to the two alternative places where the day's walk can begin, significantly aiding the extra distance and exertions that might be called on if Besse has to be reached. Rather than starting at

Bourg d'Oisans, mention has already been made in the introduction for those who might want to get to le Châtelard with their car and can therefore start there with a significant saving in altitude that would otherwise have to be climbed.

Those dependent on public transport can take the ongoing bus (incidentally, the French call their buses *cars*) from Bourg d'Oisans to the village of Huez which is about halfway up the multi-hairpinned road leading to l'Alp d'Huez (don't confuse the two). The path (clearly signposted) leaving the centre of the village cants down towards the ravine to join the route already described in the vicinity of the 'wee stone bridge', the Pont Romain. Huez is only a small place and accommodation limited. The Hotel le Gai Vallon is probably its Jewel in the Crown and to stay there it might be prudent to phone ahead to guarantee a place (tel 76 80 30 52).

DAY TWO
Clavans le Bas to la Grave

The way from **CLAVANS** leaves the village by a path that drops steeply from the centre of the village past a few gardens to reach a new roadway hairpin and bridge which crosses the Ferrand torrent. Backpackers might like to know there is a very suitable pitch just before the roadway. Once on the road, go L along it and over the bridge, ensuring you don't miss a path immediately on the L which goes steeply up the brush-covered hillside to reach the meadows just prior to **BESSE**. On a hot day the climb won't put you in the best of moods after having already come quite far enough on your first day, but - *courage!* - just think of the chilled lager that will be waiting for you in the village.

BESSE-en-OISANS has retained its 'by-gone age' image and is larger than either of the Clavans with a hotel, at least two gîte d'étapes and a campsite (tranquilly situated almost a mile 'out of town' in the 'Day Two' direction. The Hotel Alpin seems to be the focal point for village life and apart from its obvious attraction, it is here that the campsite fees are payable.

The way ahead is very pleasant and a day to look forward to. Once through the length of the main street open country is the theme. The road narrows onto a level track which dips to cross a stream to the R and then continues on the flank until beginning numerous zig-zags up a couple of shoulders. Curving to the L you eventually reach a pass which appears unnamed in the maps and available literature, but which is understood to be **COL BICHET**. Ahead the immediate terrain dips to form an enormous marshy bowl which is bordered on the far side by a rocky shelf known as Plateau d'Emparis. Beyond that is the northernmost section of the massif d'Écrins: the most prominent feature being the peak known as la Meije which at 3982m is one of the highest in the range. The ice-field on its right is Glacier de la Girose and the one nearer is the

DAY TWO
CLAVANS le BAS to la GRAVE

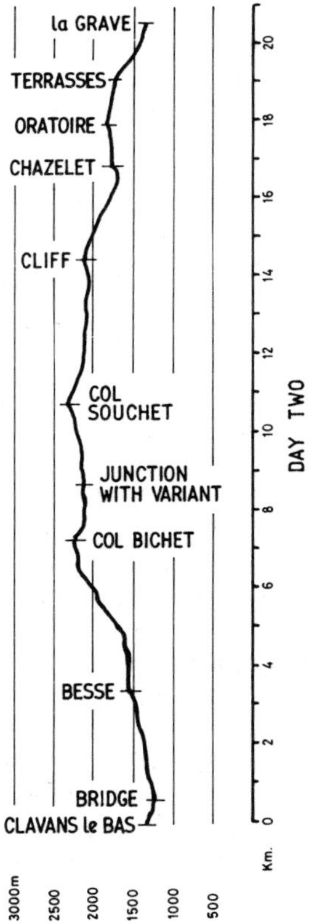

DAY TWO
CLAVANS le BAS to la GRAVE
7h.25m 21km

	Timings Sectional	Timings Accumul-tive	Altitude in metres	Ascent & Descent
CLAVANS le BAS			1368	
	0.10	0.10		− 98
Bridge			1270	
	1.10	1.20		+280
BESSE-en-OISANS			1550	
	2.10	3.30		+717 − 22
Col BICHET			2245	
	0.35	4.05		− 55
Path Junction			2190	
	0.30	4.35		+172
Col de SOUCHET			2362	
	1.50	6.25		+ 47 −623
Le CHAZELET			1786	
	0.15	6.40		+ 54
ORATOIRE du CHAZELET			1840	
	0.15	6.55		− 58
Les TERRASSES			1782	
	0.30	7.25		−301
La GRAVE			1481	

Total ascent: 1270
descent: 1157

glacier de Mont-de-Lans.

A track traverses the col and if you turn L and proceed to stroll along it you will reach in 10min the refuge known as **Chalet le Toit Pointu** (translates as 'pointed roof', which is certainly its distinguishing feature). This could be a very important staging post, having snacks available throughout the day as well as substantial lunches and evening meals along with dormitory-style accommodation.

From here it is best to descend to the barracks-looking building and then turn R to skirt the bowl and head ESE to the **junction** of paths where the GR54 variant from Mizoën meets the route you are walking. This is where the stream exits from the basin.

Continue past the junction, ascending the track beaten over the grassy slopes until reaching **COL SOUCHET**. This is probably as nice a place as any to relax awhile (brew the tea and let the feet recover?) permitting the grandiose scenery to be studied with a certain degree of leisure.

The path from here dips for a short while, then traverses grassy curving hillsides until reaching the shelf which overlooks le Chazelet. All the way you will be able to appreciate the wondrous scenery on the R, the 'balcony' path being without difficulty. You then have to negotiate steep but well-established paths to reach the small bridge crossing the Gâ. The village is then just up a taunting bit of roadway. This whole stretch usually has plenty of day visitors who head for the two attractive lakes near the col Souchet in the rocky traps of Plateau d'Emparis (see Day 15) so you might have a lot of 'bonjour' exchanges with these people as they pass.

Le CHAZELET has at least one hotel, a restaurant and two bars. If you like draught beer then ask for *la Pression*. There are two little stores as well. From the village proceed up the side of the inclined road to the well-known Oratoire du Chazelet at the promontory. This small shrine is photographed endlessly, serving as foreground in many pictures depicting the spires of the Meije behind.

Just past this distinctive spot, go R off the road at its crest and slant down towards **les Terrasse**. Take care to observe the well-painted waymarks that beckon you past the columned church entrance and onto the path heading through the pastures to issue at

Oratoire du Chazelet and la Meije

la GRAVE where there are numerous hotels, a gîte d'étape, campsite, restaurants, cafés, bars, shops, and ice-cream parlours, PTT and tourist office. Infrequent but daily buses in both directions along the valley - back towards Bourg d'Oisans and Grenoble and serving Monêtier-les-Bains and Briançon in the other direction.

There are two campsites at la Grave and the one recommended is just to the R once over the river having left the village on GR54 as described at the start of the Day Three section.

The tourist office is usually well worth a visit, generally having a display that relates to the National Park you are about to enter, providing some most interesting information.

Footnote: the position of col Bichet on the two recommended maps and as observed in other literature is indicated as 'Chalet Josserand' which, according to the guardian of the refuge Chalet le Toit Pointu, has long-since ceased to exist.

DAY THREE
La Grave to Monêtier-les-Bains

The way from **La GRAVE** is found by taking the slip-road at the higher NE end of the village: this leads down towards the river and once over the bridge at the campsite turn sharp L. Going through thin woodland the path has to gain height to get over an enormous shoulder. At its crest, the path reaches a wire fence - go through the gate and then straight ahead, ignoring the path to R alongside the fence. This correct path then leads down through tranquil woodland until reaching the river at a spot where there is a narrow footbridge giving access to the village of **Villar-d'Arêne**. Unless you want to visit the place it is not necessary to go over as the path continues on the R of the flowing water, keeping next to it for a long while.

This stretch will be found to be extremely attractive, the proximity and sight of the river Romanche being enchanting. The path goes so near the water that in places it could be impossible to make progress in flood conditions: it would then be sensible to return to Villar-d'Arêne and proceed by the roadway that runs along the opposite bank.

Turn R immediately after crossing a bridge and walk along the roadway until encountering a large campsite from which it will be prudent to fill the water container. Deposit any refuse that you might have, because the next few paces take you into the PARC NATIONAL DES ÉCRINS and you will be unable to get rid of anything once within its boundaries. Even at mountain huts, as you will discover, it will be impossible to use their bins for **your** junk as you will be directed to take it to the valley for disposal. It is for this reason that large bins are located at the entrance/exit.

The obvious path meanders along the bush-strewn and silt-covered valley floor with the river over to the R, but don't overlook the alternative about 10m up the side of the slope on the L. They

DAY THREE
La GRAVE to MONÊTIER-les-BAINS

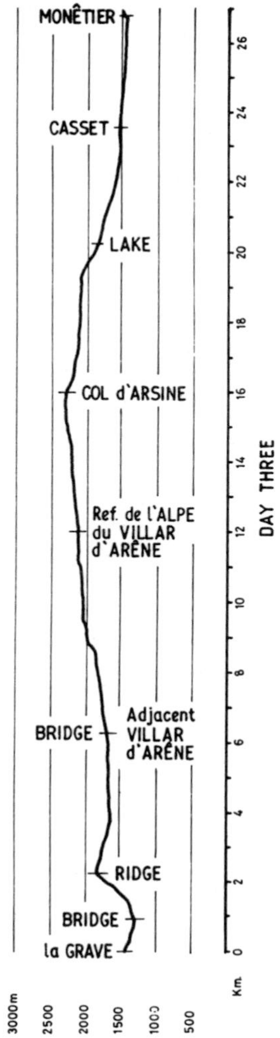

DAY THREE
La GRAVE to MONÊTIER-les-BAINS
7h.35m 27km

	Timings Sectional	Timings Accumulative	Altitude in metres	Ascent & Descent
La Grave			1481	
	0.45	0.45		+295 − 36
Ridge			1740	
	0.25	1.10		−130
Bridge (VILLAR d'ARÊNE)			1610	
	0.50	2.00		+ 57
Campsite			1667	
	1.50	3.50		+424 - 12
Ref. de l'ALPE de VILLAR d'ARÊNE			2079	
	1.10	5.00		+269
Col d'ARSINE			2348	
	1.05	6.05		−447
Lac de la DOUCHE			1901	
	0.50	6.55		−389
Le CASSET			1512	
	0.40	7.35		+ 20 − 37
MONÊTIER-les-BAINS			1495	- -

Total ascent: 1065
descent: 1051

View above la Grave with la Meije

eventually meet a boulder-covered area at their far end. Slant upwards R to encounter a spectacular waterfall, cross over at a small bridge towards it and then climb steeply for what seems ages up a promontory to its L. The steepness lessens to become more manageable, flattening as it is joined by the path from the col du Lauteret. The path goes straight over the grass-covered terrain and it will be necessary to veer off R to reach the **refuge de l'Alpe du Villar-d'Arêne**. The premises are on the edge of a cliff which faces SW into a deep side valley which is the birthplace of the river Romanche. The dominating mountain is la Grande Ruine.

Lunches, snacks and an assortment of drinks are available. After partaking in your choice of these, you have to regain the original path, but not necessarily by the way you came. Try to head off diagonally in the general direction wanted, following the odd waymark and by going up a narrow divide in the rocks. This scant path encounters marshy ground and small streams which should be very easy to cross, not re-joining the main path until much later. Very, very pretty.

It rakes upwards to the R curving L while your gaze is drawn to the gigantic pile of rocks forming the terminal moraine of the glacier d'Arsine, spilling equally into the valley you are about to depart and the one being entered. **COL d'ARSINE** is a gently curved and easily crossed high spot of the day, leading quickly down to a few small lakes that are fed with the melt waters of the glacier. Just a little lower down, look out for a small rocky island in the middle of the river which seems to be packed solid with numerous specimens of alpine flowers and plants. Further on, the indigenous rocks are an attractive dull green - a relief from the 101 shades of grey seen elsewhere.

The path then plummets, steeply zig-zagging. The signs at the head of this drop request you to keep to the formed path and not to take any short-cuts - advice which probably aims to keep erosion in check as well as to protect your ankles. It eventually levels to cross a small waterfall before finally descending to the shoreline of the small and shallow lac de la Douche. The torrent in this valley is the Petit Tabuc.

Now in graceful woodland the path lowers to reach a bridge and car park roadhead. The road is then not unpleasant to follow although its turns can be short-cut at one or two places. It emerges from the trees to cross a narrow stretch of meadowland, exiting from the National Park, before getting to **le Casset** where there is a hotel, gîte d'étape, restaurant, bar and shop. Camping is possible.

Cross the river, turning immediately R to go through the village, then exit by crossing R over another bridge which is adjacent to the bar 'Chez Finette'. Once over, turn L to traverse the field on a path which diverges from the river slightly and then develops into a satisfying stroll through camping areas. Drawing parallel to the river, it leads to a bridge which you must cross and then turn R to follow the bank at it curves round the edge of some meadows to get to another bridge. The river giving you company all this while is called the Guisane.

Don't cross this bridge, though, but turn L onto its road to reach the centre of **MONÊTIER-les-BAINS**. This is a large village, comprising several hotels, dortoir, shops and PTT. There is a bus service to la Grave/Bourg d'Oisans/Grenoble in one direction and Briançon in the other. There are many restaurants from which to choose, one of which specialises in pizzas. Mention must also be made of their swimming pool and an hour spent in this might appeal to you.

Supposing -just supposing - you wanted to have a day off at this section of the holiday, an idea to consider might be to go by bus to Briançon. This is a large town of very unusual character and to stroll its streets would be a very interesting experience being both rewarding and enjoyable.

You will find this valley very wide along its floor, fertile crops of many kinds being nurtured. The characteristic impression will be the lengthy views of the flanking hillsides. Looking SE down the centre of the valley it is sometimes possible to recognise the conical shape of Monte Viso, some 55km (36 miles) distant, just over the frontier in Italy.

DAY FOUR
Monêtier-les-Bains to Ailefroide

Leaving **MONÊTIER-les-BAINS** go back down the road to cross the bridge, turn L when over and walk a short distance to where there is another bridge. Turn R when near it to go up a narrow road which bisects meadows. Where this reaches the top end of the fields it curves R, then swings L. A few paces later take a footpath on the R which is waymarked and enter the National Park confines once again to climb through forest, quite steeply in places. It is a lovely path, though, clearly waymarked where alternatives occur, and it eventually emerges into a hanging valley through which the narrow Torrent de la Selle winds its way through an attractive glade, possibly an ideal spot to linger.

The trail continues for some while up the LHS of the clear-running water, after which it veers to the L and reaches an intrusive teleski complex which is passed to reveal more open terrain ahead, gaining still more altitude until drawing up to the rounded **COL de l'EYCHAUDA**.

There are some superb views back over to the hillsides flanking NE of Monêtier as well as the new scenery ahead. The path from here descends slowly over the LH slopes until reaching a combe down which it has scoured numerous and lengthy zig-zags into the hillside which will take what seems an age to follow. Reaching the valley floor at a bridge crossing the shallow torrent de l'Eychauda, it encounters a dirt road and meanders alongside this until reaching the buvette building at **Chambran**. A buvette is described in the French dictionary as being a 'tap room, a 3rd-class railway refreshment room' but many little shacks around the Alps have this as a label, serving teas, coffees, fizzy drinks, wine and beer. Such a place will be found here, too, with tables outside suitable for picnicking with any food brought along.

Follow the road along the length where it is level to where it

DAY FOUR
MONÊTIER-les-BAINS to AILEFROIDE

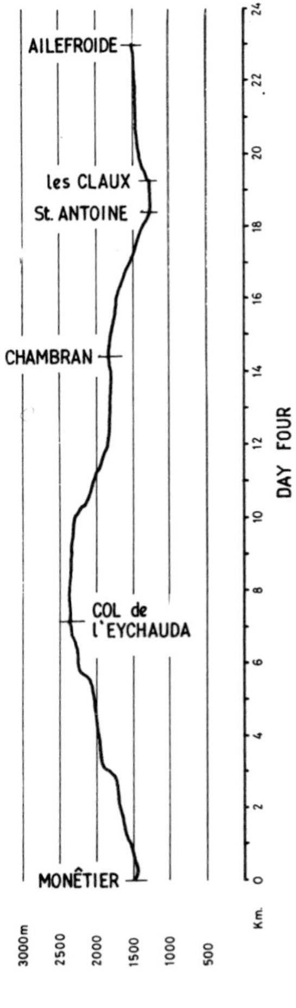

DAY FOUR

MONÊTIER-les-BAINS to AILEFROIDE

7h.30m 23km

	Timings Sectional	Accumula-tive	Altitude in metres	Ascent & Descent
MONÊTIER les BAINS			1495	
	3.10	3.10		+957 – 27
Col de l'EYCHAUDA			2425	
	1.30	4.40		–706
CHAMBRAN			1719	
	1.20	6.00		–483
St.ANTOINE			1236	
	0.15	6.15		+ 27
Les CLAUX			1263	
	1.15	7.30		+243
AILEFROIDE			1506	

Total ascent: 1227
descent: 1216

starts to dip and then watch out for a path going off R that loses height slightly quicker than the road. Where it encounters the road again, keep on the road to the next hairpin where the path continues straight on. When it again joins the road, go L then take a path almost immediately on the R. These paths are flanked by dense undergrowth and in places accompany a small but fast-flowing *bisse* which is a diverted water flow that is tapped off occasionally to irrigate the fields below. The path eventually encounters a roadhead above **St Antoine** so follow this down to enter the village where there are hotels, restaurants, bars, PTT. Here you must make a decision: according to the time at your disposal, is a diversion up to Ailefroide feasible? Whilst it will add a day to your itinerary, the author strongly recommends a visit to this village as it is a place truly of the mountains and suggests that your Tour will not be complete without a memory of this attractive spot. If you really haven't got the time then it cannot be helped, in which case you must go down the valley to Vallouise (see Day Five), ignoring the remainder of this chapter.

Go up the road to the adjacent village, **les Claux**, where you will see at its top end a large pipe coming down the mountainside to where the road disappears into a tunnel - the path starts on R just there. This will be found to be a particularly pleasant path, broad at first with plenty of atmosphere. Its arrival at **AILEFROIDE** fetches you onto the roadway next to the village store. The heart of the village is to be found L over the bridge but an efficiently run gîte d'étape is facing where meals are available even to the non-resident. The village boasts a most magnificent campsite, to be found at its lower end. The bureau is very busy during the early evening, but you will have to present your credentials and pre-pay should you wish to avail yourself of its amenities. Camping elsewhere seems to be prohibited, but you will see there are quite a few hotels that could be of service if that is your need. There is a PTT and little else unless you count the couple of souvenir shops. There seems to be quite a choice of eating places and bar/café establishments.

Waymark

DAY FIVE
Ailefroide to ref. Cézanne then to Vallouise

The author stayed at the **AILEFROIDE** campsite, having eaten at the dortoir which is where breakfast was taken on the way past in the morning before setting off towards the roadhead at Pré de Mme Carle, the situation of the **refuge Cézanne**. Where the road began to snake, a path was found that gained the same altitude in a much more agreeable manner: attractive bushes, mossy rocks and small waterfalls. The cars - together with their noise - were thrown left and far to the right as they rose up the valley, mostly unnoticed. The river is the St Pierre.

Having got to level ground, it is necessary to stay on the road for the remainder of the walk. Cross the river with it, then along the lengthy level stretch, where, hidden from view in the only cluster of trees that can be seen straight ahead will be found the refuge building. It is possible to pass nights here, but maybe all you want from the place will be the services of the caféteria? It is feasible to saunter off on either of the two main paths leading respectively towards the glacier Noire (rock debris covered) or the glacier Blanc (cleaner ice and, it would seem, the favourite - the refuge Glacier Blanc 2550m being an additional attraction).

Eventually it will be necessary to retrace your steps. Having possibly repossessed heavier items left at the campsite, gîte d'étape or hotel it might be just nice time for a light lunch. The day is relatively 'easy', aiming to put you in a good position for the commencement of Day Six, so there is no rush. You already know where the path departs the village, but even though it is familiar ground you should discover some fresh aspect to appreciate. The sun will probably be at a different angle and the change of cloud formation from the previous day will present the surroundings in different perspective.

When reaching the road at **les Claux** there will be the temptation

DAY FIVE

AILEFROIDE to ref. CÉZANNE then to VALLOUISE

5h.40m 17km

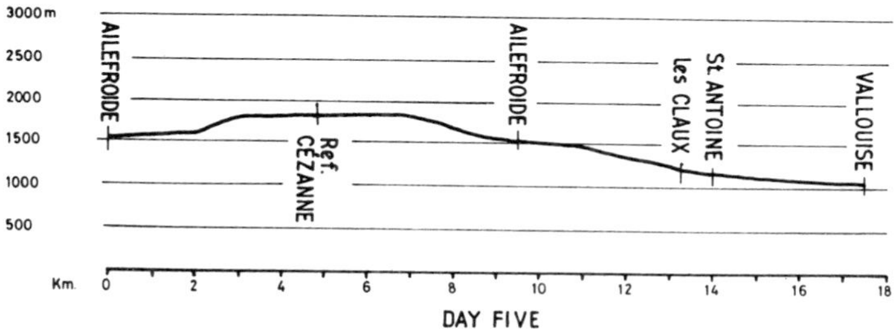

	Timings Sectional	Accumul-ative	Altitude in metres	Ascent & Decent
AILEFROIDE			1506	
	1.25	1.25		+368
Ref. CÉZANNE			1874	
	1.10	2.35		−368
AILEFROIDE			1506	
	1.10	3.45		−243
Les CLAUX			1263	
	0.15	4.00		− 27
St.ANTOINE			1236	
	1.40	5.40		+ 6
				− 76
VALLOUISE			1166	

Total ascent: 374
descent: 714

to continue on it all the way to Vallouise but those who have done this have commented on its hazardous character. Better, by far, to double back down the slip road at **St Antoine** to gain the opposite bank of the river Gyr, turning L to follow a path for the remainder of the way.

VALLOUISE has hotels, a gîte d'étape, restaurants, shops, PTT and a large municipal campsite. Buses link the village with Briançon where trains run to Grenoble and other destinations, as well as the bus service to la Grave and Bourg d'Oisans. If you are dependent on acquiring accommodation to pass the night then you cannot continue beyond this large place, but if a tent is being carried then do try to proceed some way towards Entre-les-Aigues (see Day Six). Bear in mind that you will be unable to obtain provisions until reaching Chapelle-en-Valgaudemar, so make good use of the small supermarket before passing through.

It is possible to obtain a minibus as far as the roadhead at Entre-les-Aigues. For on-the-spot details, enquire at the dortoir associated with the Hotel Edelweis.

Farmhouse, Vallouise

DAY SIX
Vallouise to ref. du Pré de la Chaumette

Taken the whole distance this is a long and strenuous section to complete. There are no places of shelter along the route either, unless you consider the miniature cab du Jas Lacroix which can only hold very few people. As mentioned in the text for Day Five, do try to make some determined effort to get a few kilometres under foot from **VALLOUISE** if you are independent.

The 1:25,000 and 1:50,000 maps are at variance in labelling the GR54 route from Vallouise to Entre-les-Aigues. The former has it on the S side of the river Gerendoine whereas the latter shows it along the road on the N. The author attempted it along the south and this had many attractions (notably the proximity to the lovely river) but difficulties were encountered on the 'middle third' which made the going unpleasant. It was particularly dangerous in traversing an avalanche-strewn ravine just prior to Prat du Clot, where dense undergrowth forces people over to the north side at Béassac where there is a small chapel but nothing else. The river crossing was made feasible by a damaged footbridge that was hardly likely to survive the ravages of another winter. There are good pitches of limited size on both sides of the river just there and it is where the author contentedly spent the night.

On balance then, to save 'road' all the way, proceed from Vallouise to encounter the river at alt 1164m, cross the bridge and turn immediately R. The path hugs the river for about 40min whereupon you should come into a fairly large wooded campsite. return to the N bank, then continue west by way of the road. Referring once more to the backpacker, the author noticed some likely-looking fields on L of the roadway just prior to Entre-les-Aigues. One of the author's friends made an overnight at the refuge des Bans 2076m up the valley biassed to the R, but you must judge for yourself if you consider this to be an advantageous staging post.

DAY SIX
VALLOUISE to ref. du Pré de la CHAUMETTE

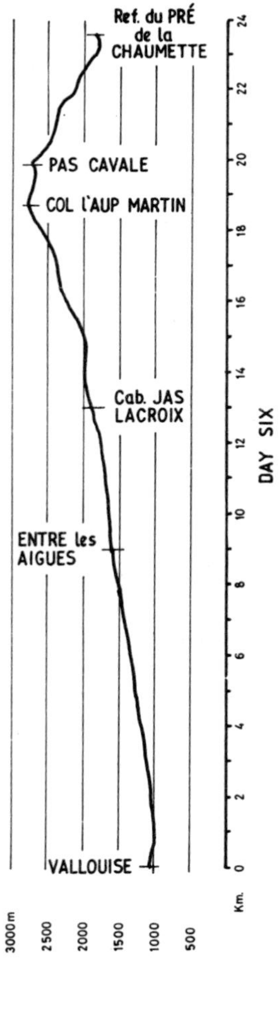

DAY SIX

VALLOUISE to ref. du Pré de la CHAUMETTE

9h.35m 24km

	Timings Sectional	Timings Accumulative	Altitude in metres	Ascent & Descent
VALLOUISE			1166	
	2.50	2.50		+ 449
Entre-les-AIGUES			1615	
	1.30	4.20		+ 331
Cab. du JAS LACROIX			1946	
	2.50	7.10		+ 832
Col de l'AUP MARTIN			2761	– 17
	0.15	7.25		+ 20
Pas de la CAVALE			2735	– 46
	2.10	9.35		+ 22
Ref. du PRÉ de la CHAUMETTE			1790	– 967
			Total ascent:	1654
			descent:	1030

There are two buildings at **Entre-les-Aigues**, probably military-owned, but of no apparent service to the rambler. Go L before these to cross a triangular area that is obviously ravaged by melt-waters as the snow-line recedes with the heat of approaching summer. Over the footbridge and then half L through this scantily-bushed no-man's land. At the trees turn L at the start of a very good path whose gradient is slight but consistent. It is very attractive and will take over an hour to draw level with the surprisingly small **cab du Jas Lacroix**. Past this place, which is almost hidden amongst large boulders, the vista begins to open out. The torrent of the Selle is delightful company as it goes about its business of tumbling towards the valley floor. Go over the river coming from the enormous combe on the R and with a few zig-zags surmount the next gigantic terrace following the well-worn path. Over another stream with a sharp LH turn you begin to experience the exposed severity of the final approach to **COL de l'AUP MARTIN**. This is the highest point encountered on the GR54 but to attain it caution has to be exercised with the final zig-zags comprised of very narrow ledges hewn from compacted slippery black shale dust.

Once at the col another world is on show: the glorious valley coming up from L with its flanks possibly glistening in the noon-day sunshine. It is around the valleyhead that the contouring path continues, initially to sharp R, to reach the **PAS de la CAVALE** whereupon yet another surprise. Overcast and raining profusely by this time on the author's visit, the varied conglomeration of ridges could nevertheless be detected and appreciated. The way down is a bit challenging at first but considered safe, although any late snow would certainly add to the difficulty. The path is steep for the bulk of the descent, levelling only to cross a small torrent, the Drac, then up for about 50 paces to be greeted at the relatively new **REF du PRÉ de la CHAUMETTE**.

Perhaps unavoidably, some literature still uses the name of the older refuge - cab Pastorale de Champoléon - to locate the spot. No matter what it is called, a truly welcome sight after three hours of lashing rain! Substantial evening meals are usually on offer and the sleeping areas nicely divided to go part-way in assuring an undisturbed night's rest.

Farmhouse at le Casset (Day 7)
Defile leading to Col de Côte Belle (Day 10)

Above lac Lauvitel (Day 13)
Barrage de Chambon and Mizoën (Day 14)

DAY SEVEN
Ref. Chaumette to Chapelle-en-Valgaudemar

This really is a 'long' day to recommend to the average walker, but the prize in reaching Chapelle-en-Valgaudemar is the prospect of a two-night stay in one of the nicest alpine situation. Anyone not responding to this idea might like to consider an overnight at ref de Vallonpierre (tenting possible) and occupy Day Eight by continuing past Chapelle to the next village (equally attractive), Villar-Loubière, which is as good a place as any to springboard into Day Nine.

The bad weather appeared to have concentrated every walker in the vicinity into the **refuge CHAUMETTE** and the breakfast room was bustling with activity. Like sheep, the various departees followed in the tracks of those preceding them on the path heading NNE. This is the way you must go, too. Gaining altitude slowly at first through rock-strewn terrain, the path curves L to get up above the terrace there and then determinedly gets higher. At a couple of exposed spots it is possible to oversee the deep valley on the L in which the refuge sits. To the R, enormous ribs of jagged rock strike an awesome spectacle. Continuing further, a little hand-work is called for in surmounting a few rocky pitches but care rather than skill is required. A final scar takes you to the first of three successive passes, the **COL de la VALLETTE**.

From here the first 10min or so of the descent can be quite precarious and should be undertaken with due caution. Once past the difficulty, you will be bound to agree that this is a particularly attractive part of the Écrins, reminiscent perhaps of the best Scottish glens. The path dips to cross an enormous bowl, passing a small lake before beginning the easy and gradual ascent to reach the **COL de GOUIRAN** for yet more spectacular scenery.

The path goes down to the R, levelling to curve above the basin floor. The slopes coming down from the right are like gigantic black fingers, scourged by centuries of rainfall. In some places the path

DAY SEVEN
Ref. du Pré de la CHAUMETTE to LA CHAPELLE-en-VALGAUDEMAR

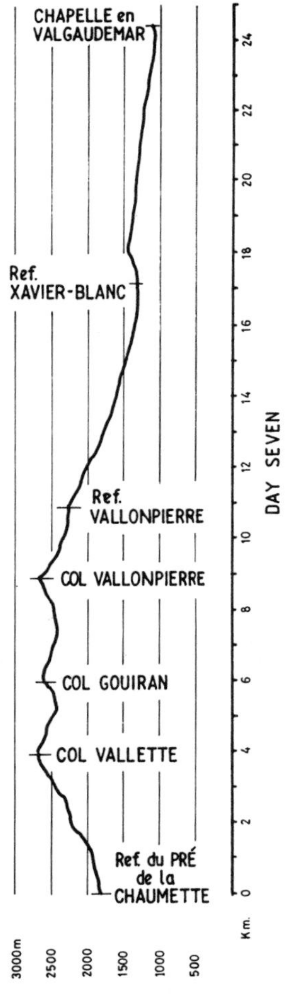

DAY SEVEN

Ref. du Pré de la CHAUMETTE to LA CHAPELLE-en-VALGAUDEMAR

8h.35m 25km

	Timings Sectional	Timings Accumulative	Altitude in metres	Ascent & Descent
Ref. du PRÉ de la CHAUMETTE			1790	
	2.15	2.15		+878
Col de la VALLETTE			2668	
	0.40	2.55		+105 −176
Col de GOUIRAN				
	0.55	3.50	2597	+270 −260
Col de VALLONPIERRE			2607	
	0.50	4.40		−327
Ref de VALLONPIERRE			2280	
	2.00	6.40		−883
Ref. XAVIER BLANC			1397	
	1.30	8.10		+ 19 −281
Le CASSET			1135	
	0.25	8.35		+ 9 − 44
La CHAPELLE-en-VALGAUDEMAR			1100	

Total ascent: 1281
descent: 1971

has eroded, creating several awkward and slippery patches, though nothing that a held breath and a few ungainly body movements can't overcome.

At these and several other stretches a walking stick will earn its keep by giving a more confident stance. The path then zig-zags up one of the larger 'fingers' to attain the **COL de VALLONPIERRE.** Narrow and bleak, you won't want to linger here if there's anything stronger than a slight breeze. Looking to the R will show the picturesque aspect of the mountain called le Sirac -probably one of the nicest viewpoints for it, although it dominates this corner of the massif. To the immediate N is yet another area opening for your inspection and enjoyment.

Don't go over this precipitous col without finding where the *intended* path actually starts, perhaps by going a little L once at the ridge to where there was a post. Once found, the path is quite straightforward but, even so, it will make exceptional demands on the ankle so do not hurry unduly. Over to the left you will see another exposed crag that is distinguished by the unusual green-coloured rocks, making one wish for greater geological knowledge. By this time you should be drawing close to the picturesque lac Vallonpierre and its **REFUGE.** Encouraged by an appetite created by the expended energies of the morning, the final paces will probably go unnoticed.

One of the nicest refuges encountered by the author, who, arriving just before 1.00pm was able to settle in to a really satisfying and plentiful lunch provided by the hospitable guardian couple. Happy memories are made from moments like these! In a state of semi-intoxication, it is only necessary to be directed to the commencement of the path (out of the refuge door, turn L, L again, over and between large rocks) and it is all 'automatic' from then on. This quickly becomes a super path, passing a shepherd's cottage on the LHS then down through alpine-garden-like surroundings.

Once again the tumbling waters are to be found running crystal-clear and will be marvelled at. The path levels for a while when encountering the main torrent, the buildings there being private and of no service to the passer-by. A short while further on, cross the river Séveraisse to R over bridge, then sharp L to follow it down to

Col de Vallonpierre

where it flows into the larger valley going down to the west.

You should be able to see cars going along a road up the far side of the main valley ahead. These will probably be excursionists making for the large chalet-hotel de Gioberney 1650m up to the right, but the GR54 swings to the L before getting that far, crossing a narrow bridge amidst a clump of trees.

Going along on the RH river bank through attractive woodland you will shortly come across the **ref Xavier Blanc**, a double-storey refuge with the capability of providing proper meals and adjacent camping for backpackers. Nice situation. Beware of water at the fountain in front of the refuge because it had a faded EAU NON POTABLE (water not drinkable) notice attached to it when last seen.

Continue on the path past the refuge for some 5min to where the path forks. The RH option climbs to encounter a road so take the LH alternative which becomes a very fine path which passes the cluster of buildings shown on the map as Rif du Sap, and later becomes a track. After about 1hr it comes to a campsite where turn L to cross a bridge to enter the hamlet of le Bourg, then bear R on a continuing path above the river.

After a further 30min or so you will come to a bridge (leading to le Casset, which is a charming wee cluster of buildings and most photogenic) but continue on the L bank all the way to **CHAPELLE-en-VALGAUDEMAR** with its hotels, restaurants, bars, gîte d'étapes, campsites, shops - all of which appear to be two in number, but there's just the one PTT.

DAY EIGHT
Day off in Chapelle-en-Valgaudemar

CHAPELLE-en-VALGAUDEMAR woke to one of those 'special' Alpine mornings; crisp air, sparkling-clear visibility, an atmosphere so still that you could hear the cow-bells in the next valley.

Having got round the exposed southern tip of the GR54 route, the author was quite content to rest-up for two nights in this attractive village. Not accustomed to a prolonged halt of this kind, the walker must consider the problem of 'getting going' again but in the event this didn't seem to be a limitation. Everything spick and span, laundry done, boots given attention with dubbin, well fed - the break must have had its value. The bath was an obvious luxury, but why not?

Sitting outside the hotel in their sunchairs, writing all those picture postcards and sipping coffee in the morning seemed to flash by. A stroll in the afternoon, probing the backwater with camera at the ready - the times soon goes. The odd chats with other residents or passing walkers all added up to a day well spent and then it was bed again with '06.30' dialled into the alarm trigger of the multi-function wristwatch.

You will gather that the 'day off' is highly recommended for your own consideration.

DAY NINE
Chapelle-en-Valgaudemar to le Désert

An alarm is hardly needed in a mountaineering hotel, as most people in the place are noticeably on the move, banging doors in the process. As early as 7.30am, the sun can strike along the valley with brilliant ferocity illuminating the foreground for the walk along the road from **CHAPELLE-en-VALGAUDEMAR**, where at that time of day the cars don't seem to be sufficient in number to warrant a nuisance. At a cluster of houses forming the hamlet of les Andrieux, one of them advertises 'Dortoir/Bar/Snacks'. Further on the road rises slightly, fetching GR54 to its next location, the attractive village of **VILLAR-LOUBIÈRE**. Here there's a hotel, a gîte d'étape and a small store. There is also a campsite about 1km before the village. Turn R up a lane, which winds past the houses, with plenty of waymarks to steer the course. At the upper end of the village the path start will be found and soon after joining it fork L at junction to rise up numerous hairpins to the RHS of the gorge. The path is of the same condition throughout so if you find its quality changing then perhaps you've gone past one of the sharp turns without noticing and are proceeding along a minor path.

The Parc National des Écrins literature indicates the presence of large numbers of mountain fauna, but to be frank, little was in evidence during the author's visit although marmots were often observed. The coats of these adorable creatures seemed to have an auburn or ginger tinge which made them somewhat different to their cousins seen elsewhere in the Alps. Their shrill cry of warning as you approach their playgrounds can still frighten beyond belief, especially if the mind is occupied with other things. This particular section of the GR54 had its share of marmots but the attraction here was the innumerable butterflies of all colours and sizes. Quite a lot seemed to settle onto the toe-caps of the author's boots and it seemed quite incongruous that these delicate treasures would want

Alongside river Séveraisse

DAY NINE
La CHAPELLE-en-VALGAUDEMAR to le DÉSERT

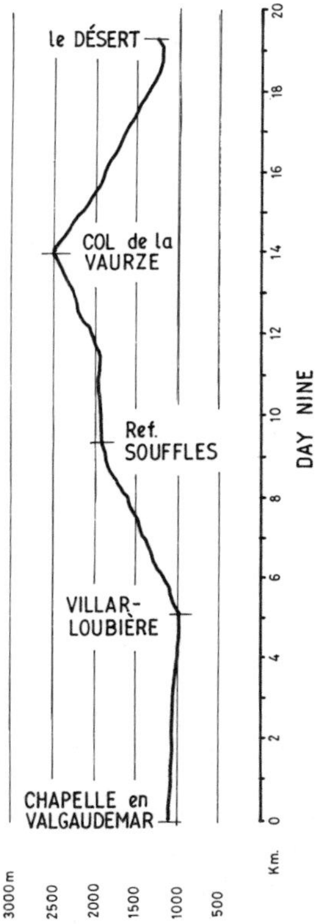

DAY NINE

La CHAPELLE-en-VALGAUDEMAR to le DÉSERT

7h.50m 19km

	Timings Sectional	Timings Accumulative	Altitude in metres	Ascent & Descent
La CHAPELLE-en-VALGAUDEMAR			1100	
	0.50	0.50		−67
VILLAR-LOUBIÈRE			1033	
	2.30	3.20		+942
Ref. des SOUFFLES			1975	
	2.10	5.30		+569 −46
Col de la VAURZE			2498	
	2.20	7.50		+18 −1261
Le DÉSERT			1255	

Total ascent: 1529
descent: 1374

to associate themselves with what is probably the ugliest item of human apparel! Then there was a solitary eagle which seemed content to soar higher and higher in the thermals of the early morning, twisting and turning in the process and putting on a fine display of aerobatics.

The 'par' for the ascent from Villar-Loubière to the refuge des Souffles is 2hr 30min and the author plodded this determinedly without halt for what proved to be a stopwatch timing of 2hr 28min 36sec. His pace at the end of the first hour was 100 in 1min 32 sec slowing to 100 in 1min 41sec at the second hour. Mention is made of this in case you want to make comparisons.

On a sloping shelf, the **Ref des SOUFFLES** was reached precisely at noon, soup then being provided by the guardian to fortify cooked meat purchased the previous evening. As is often the case, people met days before come out of the woodpile, greeting you as an old friend - friends, that is, with a common purpose. There's another way of getting to the ref des Souffles from Chapelle-en-Valgaudemar (not on the GR54 route, though) which leads straight up the mountainside to the N of the village to reach ref de l'Olan (2345m) whence the Souffles is approached by way of pas de l'Olan, col de Colombes and col des Clochettes. These others had gone that way.

The early part of the afternoon will be spent skirting the hillside in front of the refuge, gaining altitude imperceptibly until crossing a wide combe, the other side of which is scarred by the rising zig-zags which eventually lead to the **COL de la VAURZE**. This is a magnificent path, allowing excellent views over the tumbling valleys to the south and the immediate environment so rich and glorious.

Reaching the col scores up another landmark of course, but hardly prepares for the unrelenting steep drop to the next staging post. This will probably make the leg muscles scream out in complaint, notwithstanding that they are 'nicely tuned' after a week of fell-walking. For the whole descent you are able to look down upon the magical cluster of shiny-roofed houses that represent **le DÉSERT**, eventually arriving in the village after crossing a comparatively level grassy area at the valley bottom. Cross the river Bonne and then up a slope to where you will encounter the huddled buildings. Le Désert has developed for the walker and there are several places providing accommodation along with a bar where meals can be obtained in addition to a modestly-stocked store. There are numerous places that give opportunity for wild camping.

Obviously a farming community, the saving feature probably being the bar where a busy and friendly little woman will also provide a straightforward but substantial evening dinner. The outside tables are nicely positioned to capture the last of the setting sun.

Le Désert from col de la Vaurze

DAY TEN
Le Désert to Valsenestre

When at the col de la Vaurze, the view beyond the village clearly showed the defile to its north and this is the scenario for today's exercise.

Leave the upper end of **le DÉSERT** by following the narrow road, but you must turn to the L off this before it crosses the Laisse torrent issuing from the ravine you are heading for. The wide track narrows to become extremely attractive with patches of yellow and violet alpine flowers colouring the ground. The path steepens dramatically to surmount the buttress but then sweeps widely over the raking grassland, going back and forth in its determination to gain altitude.

The **Col de CÔTE-BELLE** is rounded and grassy enough to lounge about on or picnic. This is of necessity an easy day, the time and distance both being shorter than on any other section encountered, so there's the opportunity to relax. The views in both directions are very rewarding: looking backwards you will be able to see the col crossed the day before and ponder on how you coped with the descent of the steep dark face falling from it! Ahead you should be able to pinpoint the position of col de la Muzelle - the subject of Day Eleven. Binocular owners will be able to make a more detailed study and will surely conclude that its forbidding features are conspicuously off-putting.

In the absence of a breeze this is a pleasant place to linger, although descent is inevitable. The path soon skirts the gaunt pastel-brown crags flanking the tumbling N side of the col. You will be astounded at the pretty character of the bushes and foliage once a little height has been surrendered. This is a natural and outstanding alpine garden, probably at its best in the early part of the season.

When hitting the valley floor, a Y-junction is encountered. GR54 goes R to reach the approach to col de la Muzelle, but L is the way

Path sign

DAY TEN
Le DÉSERT to VALSENESTRE
4h. 40m 9km

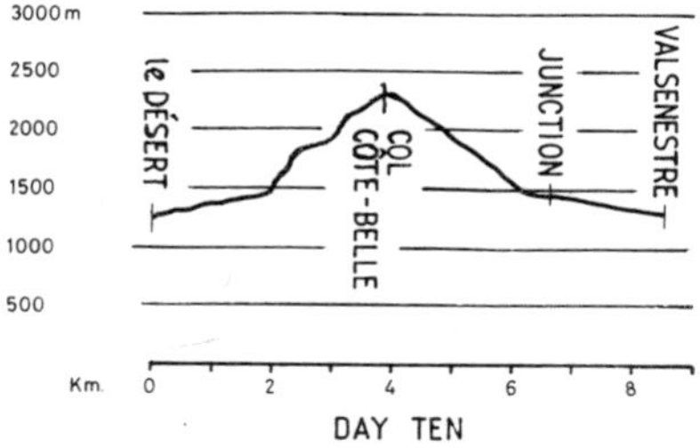

	Timings Sectional	Accumulative	Altitude in metres	Ascent & Descent
Le DÉSERT			1255	
	2.45	2.45		+ 1035
Col de CÔTE-BELLE			2290	
	1.20	4.05		− 798
Junction			1492	
	0.35	4.40		− 197
VALSENESTRE			1295	

Total ascent: 1035
descent: 995

The path from la Bérade to ref. de Carrelet (Day 12)

Plateau d'en Paris and la Meije (Day 15)

Evening in Dauphiné

At Col de Côte-Belle

to go. This pleasant wooded path - accompanied by the tumbling river Béranger - slopes down to the village of **VALSENESTRE.** Camping is not permitted until the perimeter of the National Park is passed (half-way down from the junction), where there then seems to be many idyllic pitches. The village has a gîte d'étape but little else. There is no store as such and, sad for some, no bar. However, the gîte d'étape seems to double as a café and also sells modest provisions where available. The guardian also seems prepared to provide meals and breakfasts to people who haven't slept the night there.

DAY ELEVEN
Valsenestre to Bourg d'Arud

This section has elements of grandeur about it, lovely surroundings and lush vegetation with eye-catching cascades of tumbling torrents.

Threatening the enjoyment of the day is the final approach to the col de la Muzelle. Whilst there is no denying it as a 'route' it certainly is not a 'path'. Marked with crosses on the 1:50,000 map to indicate danger, their use is entirely justified. Anyone getting this far should be fit enough to tackle the thing, but that is not the problem. The final stage is almost without grip as it progresses steeply up a compacted shaley mound. A stick is essential. In fairness, you don't see a lot of bodies at the bottom so perhaps the author is over-reacting. Why not give it an attempt? Reconnoitre the problem and see how you manage. If you find it too difficult then retreat as there is no sense in over-reaching your capabilities. There is an alternative route but even that is not without its problems (see Day Thirteen).

So, depart **VALSENESTRE** by the way you arrived to regain the path junction where branch L and follow the obvious track. This crosses a torrent to go up the LHS of the ravine, eventually ascending high above on the LH flank before levelling to cross a lengthy patch of scree to reach the foot of the difficult bit already referred to. Reaching **Col de la MUZELLE** will bring a momentary sense of relief at the accomplishment before the mind becomes occupied with other things, notably the attractive vista ahead. Looking back, you should be able to see the two previous cols, but to the N you can see the lake where the refuge is located behind its far shoreline. Beyond the lake - further away - is the winter sports complex of les Deux Alpes, straddling the curvaceous saddle descending from the main massif.

Dropping down on the N side of the col is not all that pleasant as there is no distinct path. Perhaps it is marginally preferable to slant down towards the R before encountering tracks that lead

DAY ELEVEN

VALSENESTRE to BOURG d'ARUD

7h. 10m 16km

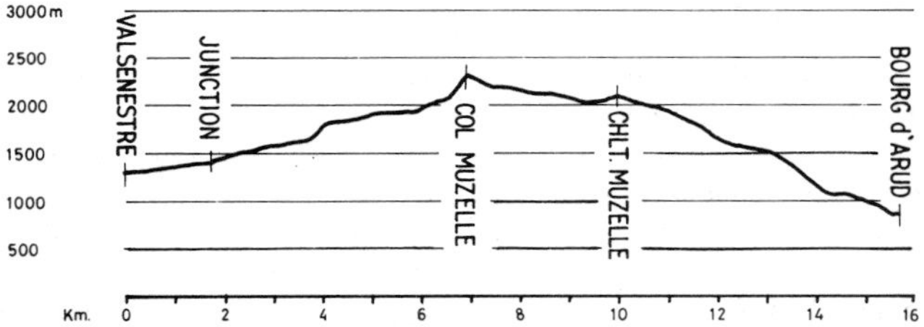

DAY ELEVEN

	Timings Sectional	Timings Accumulative	Altitude in metres	Ascent & Descent
VALSENESTRE			1295	
	0.40	0.40		+ 197
Junction			1492	
	3.10	3.50		+ 1140
Col de la MUZELLE			2625	− 7
	1.10	5.00		+ 18 − 513
Chlt. ref. de la MUZELLE			2130	
	2.05	7.05		+ 37 − 1217
L'ALLEAU			950	
	0.05	7.10		− 8
BOURG d'ARUD			942	

Total ascent: 1392
descent: 1745

inevitably to the narrow defile leading towards the lakeside.

The **Ref de la MUZELLE** is nicely situated, allowing its visitors to gaze from its balcony over the lake and up to the col just crossed as well as viewing the small glacier hanging on its left. A favourite spot for fishermen, apparently, and a convenient overnight for those who wish to lodge there. As with most other refuges, the guardian will prepare hot snacks like omelettes or soup on demand and this might be all that is wanted to bridge the gap until the time for a bigger evening meal arrives.

When leaving the refuge, go up slightly to get over the mound behind it. This leads to a marshy area, after which the wide, well-maintained path lowers itself gently into a ravine. It levels just before a log bridge which has to be crossed, then L over the larger torrent that comes principally from the lake out-pouring. Once over the other side, turn R and proceed down the narrow path towards the valley floor. Excellent all the way, every pace is a delight with beautiful surroundings. You will discover some elaborate and lengthy waterfalls to appreciate, possibly getting sprayed in places where the path goes too close. You will be in the company of this tumbling water for most of the descent until reaching some derelict stone buildings where the path veers away from the water and climbs ever so slightly: there is no need for concern at this, as it soon starts cutting down to get to **l'ALLEAU** where there is a campsite.

Go through this small cluster of houses by following the road and cross the large curved-girder bridge spanning the turbulent river Vénéon to finish the day at **BOURG d'ARUD** where there are two hotels, a gîte d'étape, a large campsite with its own store (restricted opening times) and an infrequent bus service which plies between Bourg d'Oisans and la Bérarde.

DAY TWELVE
Excursion to la Bérarde and Ref de Carrelet

Once at Bourg d'Arud, the job is almost done, so to speak. If you are one of the many who aim to complete the whole circuit under your own steam, then Bourg d'Oisans is only a lengthy stroll away, easily accomplished in a few hours. There might be severe blizzards at all the cols, 'impossible' weather, but that could not deter you from finishing now.

But, before 'signing yourself off', you really ought to pay a visit to la Bérarde. This is probably THE mountaineers' Mecca. Fortunately the minibus that plies the valley calls at the village, conveniently at 10.00 sharp, stopping outside the Hotel Château de la Muzelle.

This road journey is tremendously exciting. Soon after departure, it crosses by a small hydroelectric complex to gain height up the northern shoulder to reach first St Christophe-en-Oisans and then Champhorent, both busy little places, their faded colours probably looking best in the dazzling sunshine of mid-morning. Sideways glances will show vivid scenery and leave you wondering how such a precarious roadway was created, hovering so high above the riverbed.

When **La BÉRARDE** is finally reached, you will see for yourself that it is the gateway to better things. Before taking your first pace, check on return bus times: 4.45 perhaps? To occupy the hours in between how about a stroll up to the refuge de Carrelet 1908m? Go to the extent of the road which curves to the R at the head of the village underneath a 'bridge' (linking two buildings on either side) and this will develop into a mule path within moments. Immediately attractive, the path soon narrows your vision such that you are compelled to stare at the l'Ailefroide range, the peaks of which all but reach 4,000m into the sky.

It should take about 1hr to get to the refuge which is a pleasantly-positioned place allowing savage mountain scenery to be absorbed

Logs and geraniums

DAY TWELVE
EXCURSION to la BÉRARDE and ref. de CARRELET
2h. 00m 8km

	Timings Sectional	Timings Accumulative	Altitude in metres	Ascent & Descent
La BÉRARDE			1711	
	1.00	1.00		+197
Chlt. Hotel du CARRELET			1908	
	1.00	2.00		−197
La BÉRARDE			1711	

Total ascent: 197
descent: 197

from all quarters. Sitting at one of the outside tables in (hopefully!) blazing sunshine is no bad way of spending the intervening hours. Sampling the midday fare on offer can only complete the pleasure. The more active person will probably not be satisfied with lingering too long, in which case it is feasible to proceed further up the valley floor or to veer L and ascend to ref Temple Écrins (2410m).

Whole holidays can be spent 'doing things' around Bérarde. For instance, there's the northern valley to explore, leading to ref du Chatelleret (2225m) and, possibly, ref du Promontoire (3092m). Looking at the map will show a path up the side of the glacier de Bonne Pierre to the east of the village. All these things on another occasion, perhaps, or maybe you have time in hand to spend a night here?

DAY THIRTEEN
Bourg d'Arud to Bourg d'Oisans

It would take just under half a day to walk between Bourg d'Arud and Bourg d'Oisans. Between them, at la Danchère, lies access to a highly attractive valley that is well worth a probe. Being tempted up there will add dramatically to the time taken and turn it into a very long day instead.

Those intent on continuing to la Danchère without entering Bourg d'Arud are warned of a rogue path starting from l'Alleau that has enticed many walkers and wasted valuable time. Ensure that the path you take does not start to gain significant altitude and trails by the riverside (see below).

Depart **BOURG d'ARUD** by going over the bridge to adjacent l'Alleau and walk round the road bearing right until you see the path start on the R. This leads immediately into woods. Soon after, turn L at the junction then R at T-junction just afterwards. The path then accompanies the river as it imperceptively loses altitude, taking a good hour before raking up to encounter a roadway, where turn L to enter **la DANCHÈRE**. This is a marvellous little place with two rustic hotels, so obviously accommodation and a stay here would be possible. For doing the diversion already mentioned, a departure from the village here ought to be made fairly early, say 8.30, which implies a departure from Bourg d'Arud at around 7 o'clock.

Follow the road round as it curves through the village and where it passes the last houses you will see the sign for the path continuation to Bourg d'Oisans, to the R glancing along the LH edge of the meadow. You are encouraged to pass this path entrance and to continue along this road where it will soon narrow to form a good quality path, crossing yet another Écrins National Park perimeter. It weaves its way past thin trees, twisting around bushes and rocks until the imposing balcony is surmounted. The waterfall on the L

DAY THIRTEEN

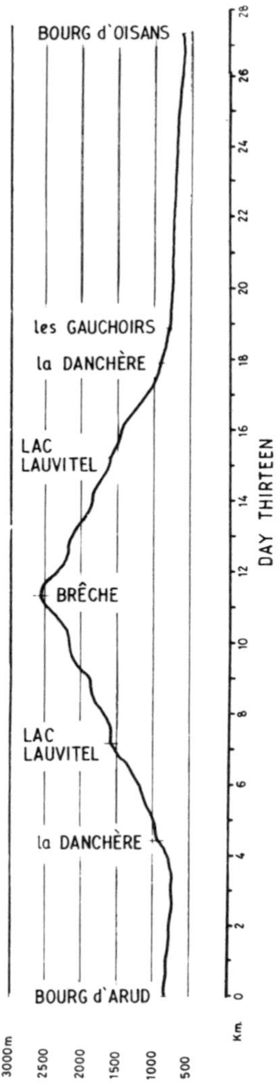

BOURG d'ARUD to BOURG d'OISANS, including diversion to BRÊCHE du PÉRIER

DAY THIRTEEN

BOURG d'ARUD to BOURG d'OISANS, including diversion to BRÊCHE du PÉRIER

11h. 25m 28km

	Timings Sectional	Timings Accumulative	Altitude in metres	Ascent & Descent
BOURG d'ARUD			942	
	0.05	0.05		+ 8
L'ALLEAU			950	
	1.25	1.30		+129 − 87
La DANCHÈRE			992	
	1.30	3.00		+548
Lac LAUVITEL			1540	
	2.40	5.40		+950
BRÊCHE du PÉRIER			2490	
	2.05	7.45		−950
Lac LAUVITEL			1540	
	1.00	8.45		−548
La DANCHÈRE			992	
	0.15	9.00		+ 17 −169
Les GAUCHOIRS			840	
	2.25	11.25		+ 18 −141
BOURG d'OISANS			717	

Total ascent: 1670
descent: 1895

Lac Lauvitel

will make you stop for a while and contemplate its majesty.

Amongst large boulders you should soon be adjacent to the attractive **lac Lauvitel**. The two buildings at its near end are privately-owned and seem to be holiday homes. Some folk are indeed fortunate! This is where a path goes L, eventually over the col du Vallon to link with GR54 at ref de la Muzelle: you may have noticed the zig-zags aiming in that direction when you were otherwise occupied on Day Eleven. But you must go along the RH shore of the lake, getting onto a narrower, but well-trod, path that soon gets higher. After leaving the trees it winds up to round a shoulder and cross a fast stream, then goes diagonally R across a large flat terrace before climbing up the R slope of the mountainside at the far end.

After that, carefully round a couple of exposed bends that allow a direct view down to the royal blue waters of lac de plan Vianney, where it then follows an easy traverse heading for the obvious pass. Or is it obvious? No - the gap with the electricity pylon is only a viewing precipice, that's why the path heads that way. You must take care to go sharp R and up at a large rock about 200 paces beforehand and where faded signs indicate 'Brêche du Périer and GR54'. Both maps show the path going to the pylon, but this is not now correct apparently. This final section to reach the col (Brêche means notch) is very steep and awkward. It would be no problem to our climbing brethren - they'd select somewhere even steeper, perhaps - but for the fell-walker a bit extreme. Likened to the final stage of the Fenêtre d'Arpette on the Mont Blanc Tour, for example, it is half the height but twice the severity.

BRÊCHE du PÉRIER might be difficult to reach but it is a delightful spot to rest and survey the next valley and the scene beyond. Looking back in the general direction from whence you have come, the near summits of the main range can now be seen. The significant icy summit is the l'Aiguille du Plat de la Selle (3596m). A few lines back 'GR54' was mentioned and it ought to be explained that this is really a GR54 'Variant'. As such it forms part of the other route from Valsenestre (avoiding col de la Muzelle) that was touched on in the text for Day Eleven.

This alternative path rises out of Valsenestre, eventually passing lac Labarre to cross near col de la Romeiou 2450. Parts of this path

Waterfall near Lac Lauvitel

can be seen from Brêche du Périer, along with its zig-zagging as it lowered itself to the floor of the intervening valley. Looks easy enough. Obviously it will have to climb to encounter the Brêche du Périer ridge several hundred paces due N where the makeshift path creeps along the western side of the rim until turning L to go over the niche. Then the walker would have to negotiate the treacherous slope already referred to.

To go from Valsenestre to la Danchère in one heave is considered by some to be a trifle too demanding, in which case there is a way of breaking the journey for those without a tent. Half way across the intervening valley there is a path which drops down to le Périer 898m, a village straddling the mountain road linking Bourg d'Oisans and la Mure. In good weather advantage might not need to be taken of this 'escape' but it is comforting knowledge for the back of the mind. For those who feel that they cannot cope with the difficulties of either the col de la Muzelle or the Brêche du Périer, it could possibly be a solution to walk along the road from le Périer to Bourg d'Oisans: very pleasant countryside, this.

For those intending to go to la Danchère via Brêche du Périer who have spent the night at le Périer village, it will obviously be necessary to retrace steps up to the path junction whence branch L to continue into the terrain already described. Still, for the person just up to the Brêche for the day, it will only be a case of turning round and to begin carefully edging down the initial slope before descending all the way to la Danchère by the route adopted earlier in the day.

At **La DANCHÈRE** there will probably be respects to pay at the local hostelry but after that the evening should be young enough to go by the path glancing down through Les Gauchoirs in the general direction of Bourg d'Oisans. The lane deteriorates into stone-covered silt for a large part of the way, crossing a stream here and there. Bear L on the two occasions you encounter a road and eventually the resort of **Bourg d'OISANS** will be within your grasp. The author pitched tent amongst the thin trees well short of target, choosing to complete the trek early the next morning.

As can be seen from the timings, this would be the longest day but if the distances were too great it would be possible to stop at la Danchère.

DAY FOURTEEN
Bourg d'Arud to Mizoën

Not had enough yet? Grand, because there is plenty more to see with two or three days extra.

Having got the satisfaction of reaching Bourg d'Oisans to complete the circuit, advantage can then be taken to do another GR54 'Variant' section, this one taking two whole days. Remember the minibus that called at Bourg d'Arud at 10.00am? This departs Bourg d'Oisans at about 9.25 (check time and boarding point) and after a leisurely breakfast you might care to take this as far as Bourg d'Arud.

At **BOURG d'ARUD** take a few paces back down the road and turn R at the hotel le Grand Rochail where on its LHS a signpost shows the start of the path to les Deux Alpes. You will see it going diagonally L up the slope. You will quickly reach **VENOSC** and

L'Alpe-de-Venosc

DAY FOURTEEN
BOURG d'ARUD to MIZOËN
5h. 25m 13km

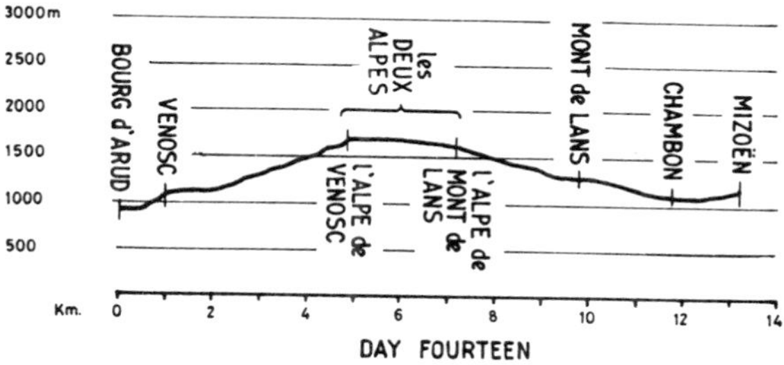

	Timings Sectional	Timings Accumulative	Altitude in metres	Ascent & Descent
BOURG d'ARUD			942	
	0.15	0.15		+ 88
VENOSC			1030	
	2.40	2.55		+ 628
ALPE-de-VENOSC			1658	
	0.30	3.25		− 6
ALPE de MONT-de-LANS			1652	
	0.55	4.20		− 370
MONT-de-LANS			1282	
	0.40	5.00		− 238
Le CHAMBON			1044	
	0.25	5.25		+ 142
MIZOËN			1186	

Total ascent: 858
descent: 614

Barn at Mizoën

recognise where the minibus called half an hour previously. Go up through the streets of the village, where there is quite an active community - hotels, restaurants, bars, gîte d'étape, PTT and shops. Skirt the church and then steeply past the houses up a stepped pavement until only the trees remain. Continue on this path as it weaves and ducks under the bubblecar-system cableway, eventually reaching the first of two resorts comprising les Deux Alpes - **ALPE-de-VENOSC**. The sun will probably have been beating relentlessly on your back for the whole ascent and so your pace won't have been too rapid, in which case your arrival will be coincident with lunch preparations at the numerous restaurants.

Before you expose yourself to the culinary delights of the place, do linger awhile at the path summit and take in the wonderful panoramic view in the general direction from whence you have just come. You will be able to see right back to the ridges crossed in the preceding days. The small niche representing col de la Muzelle can clearly be identified whereas binoculars might be needed to locate the electricity pylons adjacent to Brêche du Périer.

Not such a bad place this when out of season, several of its hotels appearing 'open' and there were several restaurants that were obviously doing a good trade. With a modicum of traffic and flags of all nations flapping in the idle breeze, the resort has a sense of activity to which the fellwalker will be unaccustomed after a fortnight in relative solitude.

Still, make use of the facilities if need be then march off N up the main street past endless chalet hotels 'this' and chalet hotels 'that' until it merges into the second of the two places, **ALPES de MONT-de-LANS**. On the R will be found the PTT and Tourist Office and, along that stretch somewhere, access to the cableway system that whisks up in several stages to the col de Jandri (3158m) which could be a good prize to grab if time and cash is available for the venture. Some people speak highly of the vista obtainable from this prestigious viewpoint.

Straight ahead, the view begins to open up. The range ahead is that over which your first two days were occupied, the gorge leading up to Clavans. As the road dips, watch out for a wide track slanting off R. This curves slightly and fetches out on the roadside just prior to the village of **MONT-de-LANS** which walk through. The road takes several more bold sweeps to reach the barrage at **Le CHAMBON**, but keep a careful lookout for a narrow path going off R just after the village which will bisect the road hairpins and give you a much more tranquil method of descent. From these slopes you should be getting increasingly vast and splendid views over lac du Chambon. Looks almost Scandinavian, don't you think?

There is a bar/restaurant immediately prior to the barrage wall. Also, the buses plying the valley call here: those serving la Grave/ Briançon and les Deux Alpes - both services go through Bourg d'Oisans.

You will be the exception if you pass right over the pavement of the dam wall without stopping for a long gaze in both directions from it. The sluice trough must be a real sight when the surplus water thrashes down it, although the reservoir side probably always looks composed, blue and calm as it maintains its general level. Immediately over the dam wall, the narrow road serving **MIZOËN** departs the N91 on its L, but there's a very steep path beforehand which cuts off the first two hairpins. It is only a short yank up to the village.

The highest spot is dominated by a magnificent little church and this is the one you could see as you descended the opposite hillside. Next to this will be found a well-run gîte d'étape whose guardian is resident in the house opposite. He appears willing to provide meals and also allows tents to be erected on the limited grassy area there. Payment is minimal but the real price of camping just there will be the sleepless night due to the hourly clock chimes from the church tower - two flimsy layers of nylon are just not capable of combating this adequately! There is a bar in the village and a modest hotel.

Cascade de la Pisse, near le Clot

DAY FIFTEEN
Mizoën to la Grave

Although this is a GR54 'Variant', the path is ABSOLUTELY splendid. There are also other attractions, about which later. The tail-end of the day will cover familiar ground, but there's no real harm in that. The aim will be to get back to Bourg d'Oisans for early evening and a convenient bus calls at la Grave at 5.45 (check!) to accomplish this.

Leaving **MIZOËN**, the way is marked just where the road turns in the centre of the village, dodging between the houses, then turns R after entering a fenced section. This curves away to reach the guard-rails of the narrow road which you join only for a few paces before going off R. Through **les Aymes** by continuing along its main thoroughfare and once outside the village branch L at an intersection. Faded path waymarks will be seen and this is an easy part to wander along. The path gradually gets more and more exposed and before the hour is up you will find it barely clinging to the rock face from whence it was hewn. Lizards were profusely in evidence, sunning themselves on the flakey grey rock slabs that have slithered down to the path edge.

Excellent sightings down to lac du Chambon here and there. Eventually the path swings up to a small lush alpage and once crossed you will encounter a sign by a stone 'archway' cairn indicating 'rif TORD' to the L, where turn. Straight ahead to **le CLOT**, but this place is an ancient shepherd's community and with no facilities for the traveller. Go and have a look as it is the subject of a restoration project. A path would then go L to link shortly with the one just mentioned.

Broad zig-zags go up the massive grass-covered hillside and bring the path up to level with a spectacular waterfall. This one is called Cascade de la Pisse and reason enough for the day's outing in its own right. Unexpectedly the path surmounts the cliff above the fall and treads the marshy ground there before striking up drier

Refuge du Fay

DAY FIFTEEN
MIZOËN to la GRAVE

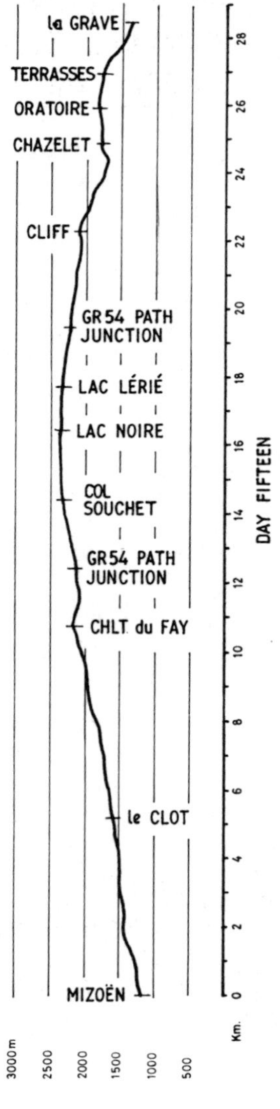

DAY FIFTEEN
MIZOËN to la GRAVE
8h. 30m 28km

	Timings Sectional	Timings Accumulative	Altitude in metres	Ascent & Descent
MIZOËN			1186	
	0.30	0.30		+110 − 16
Les AYMES			1280	
	1.20	1.50		+282 − 22
Le CLOT			1540	
	2.05	3.55		+725
Chlts. du FAY			2265	
	0.20	4.15		+ 32 −107
Path Junction			2190	
	0.30	4.45		+172
Col de SOUCHET			2362	
	0.25	0.25		+ 268
Lac NOIR			2430	
	0.15	5.25		− 50
Lac LÉRIÉ			2380	
	0.25	5.50		− 80
rejoin GR54 path			2300	
	1.40	7.30		+ 47 −561
Le CHAZELET			1786	
	0.15	7.45		+ 54
ORATOIRE du CHAZELET			1840	
	0.15	8.00		− 58
Les TERRASSES			1782	
	0.30	8.30		−301
La Grave			1481	

Total ascent: 1490
descent: 1195

Lac Noire and la Meije

terrain. Eventually it comes to the scar caused by the dusty roadway used by lorries employed on the barrage project and car-loads of weekend visitors, both of whom want effortless access to the higher pastures. The road is crossed where you will find the continuing path running parallel with it for some way as it curves round the brow.

On entering a broad defile you will see a rather splendid and large newly-constructed refuge and those who have lodged there speak well of its facilities. However, for something more intimate, some distance further up and on the L, you will find the much smaller and somewhat older refuge, the **ref du Fay**, which occupies a particularly nice corner of the world.

It's easy from here on. Down the sloping grass and over the service road - the path veers L alongside the stream to reach the path **junction**. Familiar ground? Up the GR54 on the R as it slopes towards **Col de SOUCHET**. Backward glances show the refuge Chalet le Toit Pointu, miniscular over the other side of the bowl (or 'reservoir', if it's been built in the meantime!). Upon reaching the col, seek the tracks leading R over the grass from it. When followed they lead to the two lakes, nestling at the far rim of the stony Plateau d'Emparis: lac Noire and lac Lérié.

Having a tent and pitching it adjacent to **lac Noire** is a memory the author cherishes. There was the extended face of glory over the valley - the whole range on perfect display, even a partial moon adding to the dimension. Just prior to nightfall the sheep came in their hundreds to drink from the waters and, surprisingly, anglers were there with the dawn. Cairn piles represent the location of the abutments that hover steeply above the Romanche valley and splendid views can be had from their proximity. Sleeping there makes yet another day but most people will want to reach la Grave rather than stay out. Leave lac Noire to get to **lac Lérié** by heading on tracks in the general direction of the la Meije summit. When reached bear L along its short shoreline and the rutted path you'll be on will intercept the GR54 at a point well down from the last col.

The route to la Grave from here will be fresh in your memory from the exploits of Day Two.

One further point of assistance. The bus, should you want it, halts outside the hotel 'la Maijette', roughly half-way down the main street in **la GRAVE.**

Ref du Fay

DAY SIXTEEN
Bourg d'Oisans to l'Alpe-d'Huez

The author arrived from la Grave and booked into the Beau Rivage hotel at **BOURG d'OISANS** for two nights. The reason for this was because of flight reservation strictures at Geneva. There was going to be 'a day to kill'. What to do?

The well-known Tour de France cycle race goes to various Alpine sections as part of the plan, but, almost every year the famous Bourg d'Oisans to l'Alpe-d'Huez mountain climb is fitted into the itinerary. What does it feel like for a racing cyclist to negotiate 13.5km of ascending tarmac, with its associated 21 hairpin bends and altitude difference of 1138m (3734ft)?

The author decided to do this, completely on the road (no short-cutting the corners!) and to do the whole thing without halt, just, in fact, like those competitors have to. Going from start line to finish line, his time would disgrace any cyclist but at 3hr 50min may be not all that bad for a walker.

This walking climb had many unexpected things of interest: the nice places passed through, the view over the valley and down onto the scene of the initial stages of Day One, the very welcome and excellent lunch on arrival at **l'ALPE-d'HUEZ**.

Most of the popular cyclists had their names painted on the roadway by their supporters and friends - their way of urging that extra ounce of energy which might make just that subtle difference to the winner's timings. An eerie twist this, making it easier to imagine the packed enthusiasts on either side of the road yelling their further encouragement.

Two hours 40min down - an unexpectedly pleasant day. Incidentally, a leading cyclist can reckon on about an hour for the ascent.

An idea for you, perhaps?

DAY SIXTEEN
BOURG d'OISANS to l'ALPE-d'HUEZ
6h. 30m 27km

	Timings Sectional	Timings Accumul-ative	Altitude in metres	Ascent & Descent
BOURG d'OISANS			722	
	3.50	3.50		+1138
L'ALPE-d'HUEZ			1860	
	2.40	6.30		−1138
BOURG d'OISANS			722	

Total ascent: 1138
descent: 1138

Oratoire du Chazelet, la Meije